JOHN ROMAN BAKER's early work included poetry, short stories and novels, but since 1989 he has mainly devoted himself to writing and directing for the theatre.

His plays, written from a homosexual perspective, are a unique chronicle of gay male behaviour, obsession and aspiration. AIDS, economics and social change provide the backdrop to the situations played out on stage.

He has lived and worked mainly in Paris, Amsterdam and Brighton

Other plays by the same playwright include:

In One Take

The Last Century of Desire

The Prostitution Plays

East Side Skin

Prisoners of Sex

THE CRYING CELIBATE TEARS TRILOGY

by

John Roman Baker

THE CRYING CELIBATE TEARS TRILOGY
comprises the following plays:

> Crying Celibate Tears
> The Ice Pick
> Freedom to Party.

The plays were first presented separately from 1989 to 1991. In 1992 they were presented together for the first time as part of the Brighton Festival. Given the contemporary subject matter of the work slight amendments to the original scripts were made by the playwright prior to their presentation in 1992. It is these versions which are published in this edition.

ISBN 978-1-4092-2668-0

This first edition was published by Aputheatre in 2008.

Application for public performance should be made to the playwright via the following email address:

rights@aputheatre.com   www.aputheatre.com

CRYING CELIBATE TEARS was first performed on May 22nd 1989 at the Sussex AIDS Centre, Brighton, England as part of the Brighton Festival. The play was directed by Geoffrey Colman and had the following cast:

ERIC	Andrew St John
DAVID	Tom Sharpstone
JEFF	Nigel Greenhalgh
KEITH	Graham White

THE ICE PICK was first performed on May 21st 1990 at the Marlborough Theatre, Brighton, England as part of the Brighton Festival. The production was awarded the Zap Award for Best Theatre jointly with the Satyricon Theatre of Moscow. It was directed by Robert Snell and had the following cast:

MICHAEL	Mark Laville
PETER	Nigel Fairs
MICHAEL's FATHER	Ted Dawson
ADAM	Stephen Israel
TIM	Stephen Israel
ERIC	Stephen Israel
MAN AT PARTY	Ted Dawson

FREEDOM TO PARTY was first performed on May 14th 1991 at the Marlborough Theatre, Brighton, England as part of the Brighton Festival. The play was directed by Paul Hodson and had the following cast:

MARK	Clive Perrott
SIMON	Nick Miles
ALEX	Dino G Houtas
PAUL	Simon Casson

Dedicated to all those who failed in their response to AIDS.

CRYING CELIBATE TEARS

Characters

ERIC, in his thirties

DAVID, mid to late twenties

JEFF, late twenties

KEITH, late twenties

Place

London, 1989

SCENE ONE

(Darkness. We hear music which finally incorporates the following recorded message.)

ERIC: "I'm sorry there's no one here at present, but if you would care to leave your name and telephone number, we'll get back to you as soon as possible."

(Lights gradually up. ERIC and DAVID's flat. DAVID with scrapbook, scissors and newspapers. The sound tape continues. ERIC and DAVID are unaware of it.)

Voice 1:   Hi Eric its Tom. I've just come from Paul's. He's in an awful state. Was hours trying to persuade him not to. Told him while his quality of life was good, there was no reason for such a negative thing - you know how hard it is with this quality of life thing. All the same I think I won him over to positive thinking. *(Pause.)* How long can I talk for on this machine? I hate them. Anyway I called Andrew and got him to sit with him, but I'm not sure if he's capable of coping with someone contemplating suicide. See you next week.

Voice 2: David this is Eric. The Centre has a meeting, so I won't be back until about eight-thirty. Bye for now. Wait - don't switch off. David, don't wank, it's not worth it.

Voice 3: Eric, I've been scared shitless since we nearly got caught in the park. Thanks for doing a bunk and leaving me naked in the bushes. *(Pause.)* I'm in Aberdeen off the rig and will be coming to London. Can we meet? I'll be in the pub where we first met the day after tomorrow. At six. I'll wait an hour.

(The tape finishes. Lights fully up. Long silence. ERIC looking at a magazine and DAVID cutting newspaper articles.)

ERIC: I'd like to look at some really good porn. Something different. Bit more of suggestion, less of the obvious. You're not listening. Bloody scrapbook. *(Pause.)* Still, it wouldn't do the job. I know it wouldn't however different it was. And as for the real thing. Do you remember what it was like?

DAVID: *(Picks up an article and waves it at ERIC.)* Have you read this? I'd like you to read it.

ERIC: Bloody articles.

DAVID: An HIV counsellor should read these articles. It says here you can't get the virus by sucking. Can't remember what it was like sucking.

ERIC: Precisely.

DAVID: What?

ERIC: You almost can't remember what sex was like.

DAVID: I've been afraid that certain things aren't as safe
           as they tell us.

ERIC: *(Pointing to the article.)* And does this tell you
           anything?

DAVID: It's confusing. Now it's safe, now it isn't. I'd like
           to believe sucking is safe.

ERIC: I'd tell myself I believed it, and go out and
           suck. But then that minimal risk that it was
           unsafe, that tiny "I don't know" risk might hold
           me back same as you, and I wouldn't. *(Pause.)*
           And then aren't we forgetting we are self-
           ordained celibates? Six months! Forget sucking,
           I haven't even mutually wanked.

DAVID: I wouldn't call that too long a time. I am
           irresistibly attractive and have been celibate for
           over a year and a half.

ERIC: Year! You have been celibate for just under a
           year.

DAVID: A year and a half. It will be Christmas -

ERIC: So you do remember last Christmas?

DAVID: *(Guiltily.)* Oh, that.

ERIC: That indeed! Six foot of that if I remember!

DAVID: Too boring to remember.

ERIC: Cropped black hair, leather jacket. Blue eyes. I
           remember, and so do you. *(Pause.)* A social
           worker. He'd just come off that training
           weekend. I remember him saying - it was said
           loudly because I overheard it while I was
           pouring you your favourite vodka - that he
           knew some amazing new body rubbing
           techniques, and he wanted to show you them.

(Slight pause.) I don't think he was a social worker at all. I think he was a masseur out to impress us.

DAVID: He -

ERIC: Showed you. In the bathroom. We had people pissing in the hall waiting outside while he showed you. You ruined an elegant carpet.

DAVID: He wanted to get me into the bathroom for another reason.

ERIC: To pee together?

DAVID: He was too scared to admit the real reason with people like you listening.

ERIC: The reason being?

DAVID: A sore on his leg.

ERIC: Really!!

DAVID: He had been scared to death on the training course by that over-the-top exercise in dying. You know the one where you go through dying step by step? He got panicky during the exercise because he had this purple sore, and he frightened himself into believing it was Kaposi's Sarcoma.

ERIC: So, if I'm hearing right he got you into the bathroom because he had been told you had been a male nurse? *(Slight pause.)* Until of course you went into a more lucrative line of business.

DAVID: Managing a fast-food restaurant is hardly lucrative.

ERIC: But more fun.

DAVID: Try it.

ERIC: *(Pause.)* Did he massage you well?

DAVID: No.

ERIC: I don't believe it. You came out of that
            bathroom positively glowing.

DAVID: If you're doubting me, why shouldn't I doubt
            you? It's alright you telling me you don't have
            sex, and going around with this "I am the virgin
            of the Fulham Road" image. *(Long pause.)* I bet
            you have sex.

ERIC: I do not.

DAVID: You are not the most sexually honest of people.

ERIC: Could be that I don't want anyone but you.

DAVID: *(Hears. Gets up. Paces the room.)* Maybe I'll go
            to a club. The fresh air will do me good. I'm
            suddenly tired of being cosy. Gets awfully close
            in here with just us two.

ERIC: Good idea. *(Points to the articles.)* Read them a
            few obituaries while you're there. *(Pause.)*
            Sorry. I'm bored as well. I'm playing.

DAVID: If you're that bored read some of these articles.

ERIC: Fuck Aids. *(Long pause.)* David?

DAVID: Yes?

ERIC: *(Looks at him.)*

DAVID: What?

ERIC: *(After a long pause.)* Nothing. Just put that
            scrapbook away before you go out.

BLACKOUT

SCENE TWO

(A bar. DAVID stands alone. Loud music. Pause. JEFF enters also alone. Both men stand far enough apart to be just able to hear each other.)

DAVID: You could come over and join me.

JEFF: *(Not moving or looking at him.)* Would you like a drink?

DAVID: Got a full glass. *(Glances at JEFF.)* So have you. Shall I join you?

JEFF: It's hard talking above this music.

DAVID: Who makes the first move? *(Pause. Joins JEFF.)* I make the move.

(Music fades to background.)

JEFF: Do you come here - ?

DAVID: *(Laughs.)*

JEFF: I'm sorry.

DAVID: No, don't apologise. It was cute. I haven't heard it in years.

JEFF: I'm not practised in opening lines. I don't go anywhere very often.

DAVID: That sounds sad. *(Pause.)* You don't go anywhere?

JEFF: I meant to say I don't come to these places often.

DAVID: Why?

JEFF: Oh, general wariness really. *(Pause.)* Aids and - the other.

DAVID: The other what?

JEFF: People out of work. You've got to be so careful not to meet someone who doesn't work. Gets complicated. Unequal.

DAVID: I might be out of work.

JEFF: No, you're not. I can tell. It's sort of a look people have -as if they are doing something outside of these places. For a start you don't drink enough for someone out of work. *(Pause.)* How long have you been here?

DAVID: 'bout an hour.

JEFF: You'd be half drunk by now if you were out of work. Couldn't afford it, but you would be. *(Pause.)* I've done quite a bit of character training in observing people.

DAVID: Professionally?

JEFF: Yes. I've interviewed quite a lot of people.

DAVID: *(Smiles.)* Do I get the job?

JEFF: What?

DAVID: Just a line.

(Awkward silence.)

JEFF: It's such a vacuum if you meet a guy on social security. I feel more at ease knowing someone works. *(Pause.)* I'm a systems analyst. Computers. I don't have much interest in running around. I finish work, go home, play music.

DAVID: Cosy.

JEFF: What do you do?

DAVID: I manage a fast-food restaurant.

JEFF: *(Disappointed.)* Oh.

DAVID:	It's work. And if you're wondering what I smell of it's Lagerfeld, not burgers.
JEFF:	I'm not close enough to smell you.
DAVID:	We could get closer.
JEFF:	I'm not good at passes.
DAVID:	I made a pass?
JEFF:	Sounded like one to me.
DAVID:	Naughty me then. I'm only out for a chat.
JEFF:	*(Disappointed again.)* Are you?
DAVID:	I'm trying to be faithful to a celibacy conviction. Bit redundant really as everyone else seems to have returned to fucking.
JEFF:	Can't say I've noticed.
DAVID:	Don't look so shocked. *(Pause.)* You look as if you're a bit of a celibate yourself.
JEFF:	A bit emotionally rusty.
DAVID:	Quaint way of putting it. *(Pause.)* And physically?
JEFF:	I do -
DAVID:	Do you? Good. *(Pause.)* I'm embarrassing you.
JEFF:	Yes - but you're the nicest looking person I've met in a long while.
DAVID:	That sounded like a compliment.
JEFF:	*(Awkwardly.)* It was. I don't often give guys compliments.
DAVID:	No, you don't look as if you would.
JEFF:	I'm not at ease here. Usually I go out to a dinner, or a show. *(Quickly.)* With people I

	know at work. *(Pause.)* I'm not at ease standing around here.
DAVID:	Having men trying to pick you up?
JEFF:	They don't often.
DAVID:	Maybe you don't notice.
JEFF:	They do sometimes.
DAVID:	Then what do you do?
JEFF:	I'm polite.
DAVID:	Politely cool, or politely warm? *(JEFF shuffles his feet.)* Either you're embarrassed again or you want to dance. I'll change the subject. *(Pause.)* Do you mind me having a job that's less equal than yours?
JEFF:	What a question.
DAVID:	A relevant one if we get around to arranging another meeting.
JEFF:	I don't mind your job. At least you have one.
DAVID:	Does that mean that I'll get to see you again?

BLACKOUT

SCENE THREE

(Evening. An Aids helpline. ERIC and DAVID. ERIC is waiting by a phone. DAVID takes the phone off the hook. ERIC replaces the receiver.)

ERIC:	I'm supposed to be leaving this line open for people who need to call in.
DAVID:	I need to talk.
ERIC:	We live together. Can't it wait? I'll be home in a couple of hours.

DAVID: I've had this experience. This fright.

ERIC: *(Impatiently.)* David if you're having me on. If
         this is one of your games.

DAVID: I was reading this book. First I was trying to
         have a wank.

ERIC: *(Exasperated.)* David I have serious work to do
         here. Talk to me later. *(Phone rings.
         Mockingly.)* May I? *(Picks up phone.)* The
         Centre. Can I help? *(Pause.)* Yes. Yes, you did
         the right thing. What size is it? *(Pause.)* The
         lump. *(Pause.)* The lump is where? *(Pause.)* Is
         it inflamed? Have you seen a doctor? *(Pause.)* I
         suggest you see your doctor tomorrow. *(Pause.)*
         Not your doctor. OK then, the clinic. *(Pause.)*
         No, I don't think it's Aids related, but I'm not
         here to make a diagnosis. *(Pause.)* Have you
         any reason to believe the lump on your right
         breast is Aids related? *(Pause.)* Your nipple has
         grown larger? *(Pause.)* Cancer? *(Pause.)* Yes, I
         understand your panic, but don't panic. See
         your doctor. I can't really help you on this.
         (Pause.) Of course I am here to help. *(Pause.)*
         I'm not being dismissive. I sympathize. If one
         of my nipples had grown larger - *(Pause.)* No, I
         am not an old man who does not understand.
         How old do you think I am? Sorry. Forget that.
         I shouldn't have asked that. It's been a bad night
         here. *(Pause.)* I am not giving you my
         problems. *(Long pause.)* Hello... hello... are you
         still there? *(Turns to DAVID. Replaces
         receiver.)* I just fucked up on a call because of
         you.

DAVID: By the sounds of it you weren't handling it very
         well.

ERIC: Thank you.

DAVID: Don't make me feel guilty.

ERIC: Why not? I was rude to the woman. I was rude because you make me feel edgy.

DAVID: I'm part of the public too. I have a problem, Mr Counsellor.

ERIC: Don't call me that.

DAVID: Will you please listen to me? *(Pause.)* When I at last gave up on the wank I decided to read a book. "Sex in the Soviet Union".

ERIC: Appropriate post-wank reading.

DAVID: You know I'm interested in the Soviet Union.

ERIC: God knows why. It doesn't exist anymore. *(Slight pause.)* Go on, David.

DAVID: Well, it seems this young man in Outer Siberia had this masturbation problem as well. Repression in the good old USSR had so fucked him up that he could only get his rocks off by picking up stray Siberian tomcats and then nailing them to his farmyard door.

ERIC: *(Laughs.)*

DAVID: Listen to this seriously.

ERIC: David, how can I?

DAVID: He could only come by crucifying these poor blasted moggies. He could only ejaculate by watching their death agonies.

ERIC: Look, I know we live in a country that forbids nearly all pornographic aids - if you'll pardon the word - but nobody here would be into crucifying cats to orgasm.

DAVID: It scared me.

ERIC: Because you don't like cats?

DAVID: It scared me because someone went that far to -
           well, to manage it - coming. *(Pause.)* Eric, the
           guy enjoyed it. He came off on it.

ERIC: Fear, David, can sometimes make us climax
           when all else fails. *(Pause. Smiles.)* Has this got
           anything to do with your new friend?

DAVID: He's got a cat. A tomcat moggy. He wants me
           to like that tomcat moggy. *(Pause.)* I'm sorry. I
           realise I'm being stupid.

ERIC: A bit.

DAVID: *(Seriously.)* I was afraid. *(Reaches out and
           touches ERIC.)* Someone out there went that
           far.

BLACKOUT

SCENE FOUR

*(ERIC and DAVID'S flat. Lights up. JEFF and DAVID.
Silence. JEFF is nervously looking at DAVID.)*

JEFF: What are we doing here?

DAVID: Still waiting to see who makes the first move.
           (Pause.) We've had dinner together, met in
           pubs - although you hate them - but we haven't
           been alone together.

JEFF: I don't make moves.

DAVID: You didn't really come up to see my fifties
           antiques? I mean I could ring my mother if you
           would like to see a real one. *(Looks intently at
           JEFF.)* You're more afraid to touch than I am.
           (Slight pause.) Do you ever touch?

JEFF: I had a lover for two years.

DAVID: *(Laughs.)* Then you must have at some point.
            (Pause.) Well, we are back at square one. Might
            as well be in a pub as here. And to think in
            some circles this is called a courtship ritual.

JEFF: I want to take this slowly.

DAVID: It doesn't "come" easy for either of us does it?

JEFF: I don't like vulgarity.

DAVID: Mate, snails bonk quicker than we do. *(Pause.)*
            Come on, don't look offended. Let's sit down
            next to each other.

JEFF: If I do sit down, don't do anything.

DAVID: Aids again. *(Mockingly.)* Jeff, you can't get
            Aids by touching. This is the real problem, isn't
            it? *(Pause.)* You can get scabies by touching,
            but somehow I don't think either of us has
            scabies.

(DAVID sits down. JEFF awkwardly sits next to him.)

DAVID: *(Brightly.)* Do you like games?

JEFF: I'm too old to play.

DAVID: Thought we might try a bit of trivial pursuit.

JEFF: I'm not too good. Anyway, it's better if more
            than two play.

DAVID: Yes, but two can play.

JEFF: I'm sorry, the literature questions let me down.
            I'm not a trivial pursuits person. And before you
            say it, I don't just mean the game.

DAVID: Well, if we can't play games together, let's talk
            about ourselves.

(Long silence.)

DAVID: *(Breaking the silence.)* At nine I knew what gay meant. *(JEFF remains silent.)* I let a swimming instructor touch my willy in the swimming baths.

JEFF: *(Shocked.)* You let him?

DAVID: Why not? I'd been randy since the age of seven, and was grateful someone took an interest in it.

JEFF: No one ever did that to me.

DAVID: You should have asked. *(Looks at JEFF.)* Have they since? I mean other than your lover.

JEFF: What?

DAVID: You know what. Touched your cock.

JEFF: If this is to relax me sexually...

DAVID: Sorry Jeff, I thought it was a coldly factual question. Hardly hot talk - but - if you want it hot, did you see that Spanish film where they all had lots of sex, and one of the guys who was a killer went around moaning "fuck me, fuck me" all the time? *(Pause.)* Not much hope of any of that happening to us, is there?

JEFF: Neither of us are killers.

DAVID: *(Aside.)* Or lovers.

JEFF: *(Hears.)*

DAVID: *(Pensively.)* I could be a killer. You have a cat.

JEFF: You want to kill my cat?

DAVID: Does it have balls?

JEFF: No.

DAVID: How new millennium of it. Soon none of us will have any balls.

JEFF: *(Emphatically.)* I have balls.

DAVID: Mine are atrophying. *(Smiles.)* It's really rather painful. I'm afraid that one morning I will wake up and, oh dear, they will have shrunk.

JEFF: You're sex talk obsessed.

DAVID: *(Sadly.)* I wish I was. *(Pause.)* I don't like cats. I'm allergic to them. Come out in a rash if they lick me.

JEFF: My cat doesn't lick.

DAVID: Doesn't he clean himself?

JEFF: I mean other people.

DAVID: *(Absurdly.)* He's a person?

JEFF: I mean he doesn't lick people. *(Pause.)* David, stop playing with words and making fun of me. You make fun of me most of the time. You can't see it, can you? No one sees it.

DAVID: What?

(Silence.)

JEFF: I'm crying inside.

(Silence.)

DAVID: *(Coldly.)* Shed tears then.

JEFF: You're a hard bastard.

DAVID: "Hard" is not a word either of us should be using.

JEFF: Get off sex.

DAVID: *(Pause.)* Why won't you let me kiss you?

JEFF: I did. You did.

DAVID: You had your lips closed tight.

JEFF: I never open my mouth to kiss these days.

DAVID: These days. What a glorious cliché that has
          become. These days I don't go out cruising any
          more.

JEFF: Then how did we meet?

DAVID: We didn't cruise. We met with all the politeness
          of a Victorian novel. *(Pause.)* These days I
          don't go down to Brighton any more. These
          days - it's the opening for a song really.

JEFF: Don't be cynical. Suits you too much.

DAVID: Seriously, what do we do? I mean, we all seem
          to watch a lot of television. Do in this house
          anyway. "Blind Date". I like the fellas. It's the
          nearest a lot of us will ever get to promiscuity.
          Meeting people blind, then chucking them over.
          Anyway, it's nice seeing people meeting people.

JEFF: You met me.

DAVID: That's true.

JEFF: Regret it?

DAVID: I thought of sex when I looked at you.

JEFF: *(Looks.)*

DAVID: Yes, that again. It's on my mind. I have a
          rampant mind.

JEFF: It's on my mind too.

DAVID: Seems we have something in common.

JEFF: You try too hard to be smart.

DAVID: It's a defense mechanism.

JEFF: It's off-putting. *(Pause.)* I want to talk to you
          about so many things.

DAVID: Like why I manage a fast-food restaurant?

JEFF: We could talk about jobs. Most people do.

DAVID: I'm not ambitious.

JEFF: I like my job.

DAVID: Glad you do. *(Pause.)* I don't like mine.
           (Pause.) So you want us to have serious talks
           and things?

JEFF: It would be normal.

DAVID: Take our minds off sex, eh? *(Pause)* Let's hope
           we have lots to talk about.

BLACKOUT

SCENE FIVE

*(ERIC and DAVID's flat. Evening. Several days later.
ERIC, DAVID and JEFF.)*

ERIC: Jeff, don't bite your fingernails. You're not on
           approval. You haven't been brought home to
           meet a prospective mother-in-law. *(Long
           silence. ERIC turns to DAVID.)* Does he talk?

JEFF: I talk.

ERIC: Good. For a while you had me worried. I
           thought you were stuffed.

DAVID: Eric!

ERIC: Jeff, I'm rude by nature. Handsome too they
           say, which compensates. I'm also a good
           listener to people who talk.

DAVID: That's a hint, Jeff.

JEFF: What do you want me to talk about?

ERIC: First, please, will you assure me about one
           thing?

JEFF: What?

ERIC: That you are not talking much because you are shy, and that it's not me.

JEFF: It's not you.

ERIC: *(Hopefully.)* Then you like me?

DAVID: Eric, he doesn't know you.

ERIC: Everybody likes me.

DAVID: That's not true.

ERIC: And he mustn't break the pattern. My self-esteem couldn't take it.

DAVID: *(To JEFF.)* Fortunately he's not always like this. He's nervous about meeting you, contrary to appearances.

JEFF: *(Laughs.)* That's re-assuring.

ERIC: He laughed. *(Claps his hands.)* He likes me. *(Pause. To DAVID.)* You told me Jeff likes Scotch. Why then have we only got vodka?

JEFF: I don't mind.

ERIC: You're being polite. We like to please, don't we David?

DAVID: There's some Scotch in the kitchen. I'll go and get it.

ERIC: Why are you hiding it in the kitchen?

JEFF: Don't go for me. Another vodka would be fine. There's no cause for a fuss.

ERIC: I like a fuss. It's making conversation isn't it?

JEFF: I asked for vodka if you remember.

ERIC: Only because you saw we had one bottle and it had vodka written on it. You were being polite, and David was being selfish in not thinking about you. That's my last word on the subject.

DAVID: Good.

ERIC: So what do you do, Jeff?

JEFF: Work?

ERIC: You can tell me about your playtime if you like.
         People think that because of the Centre my life
         is one long playtime.

JEFF: Do you work?

ERIC: I'm a "professional". I counsel people. And I'm
         paid for it.

JEFF: What for?

ERIC: You mean why do they pay me?

JEFF: No, what's the job for? Who do you counsel?

ERIC: People who are HIV. Relatives. Lovers.
         (Pause.) Beneath my superficial exterior I have
         an intense, committed heart. A normal heart.

DAVID: Ha ha. I'll go for that Scotch. *(Exits.)*

ERIC: You look pale, Jeff.

JEFF: I have a friend, Keith, whose lover died of
         Aids. I'm nervous around Aids. It happened
         recently.

ERIC: *(Almost flippantly.)* Well, that's a common
         feeling. Don't worry about it. I'll counsel you.
         (Moves nearer to JEFF.) I'm experienced.
         David isn't.

JEFF: David's OK.

ERIC: He and I are best friends. You are preaching to
         the converted. *(Pause.)* What do you do?

JEFF: I'm a systems analyst. Computers.

ERIC: I -

JEFF:	It usually stops talk when I say that.
ERIC:	Shouldn't really. I mean we are not all hairdressers or working for the Queen Mother anymore are we? A lot of us are now in the City, or something. *(Slight pause.)* Are you in the City?
JEFF:	Behind Covent Garden actually.
ERIC:	What a nice place to be. Do you like opera?
JEFF:	Not much.
ERIC:	Pity. I'm on more familiar ground with opera.
JEFF:	Sorry, I can't oblige.
ERIC:	Tell me about your place behind Covent Garden.
JEFF:	It's not my place. I work with at least four other people.
ERIC:	All gay?
JEFF:	Some of them.

(DAVID enters. Hands a glass of Scotch to JEFF.)

ERIC:	*(To DAVID.)* Jeff works in computers. I hope you understand more about it than I do.
DAVID:	He knows I'm living in the Nineteenth Century when they didn't have computers.
ERIC:	Ah, the Nineteenth Century. That's the time and place where all the right-minded Tories would like us to be. Imagine all those wonderfully cheap East End street boys, all giving themselves for a hot meal.
DAVID:	Sounds like today.
ERIC:	By the way, Jeff, what are your politics? If anyone new comes into the family I like to

know how they vote. An old custom we have. *(Pause.)* Tory?

JEFF: They're strong for this country. There's no one else to vote for. *(To ERIC.)* Do you vote Tory?

ERIC: Despite my posh London accent - acquired by a couple of years training with cultured Knightsbridge queens - I come from a solid working class labour voting family. I've done everything in my power not to be like them. *(Pause.)* Yes, I do. Tory.

DAVID: I hate Tories.

ERIC: *(Pretending astonishment.)* Pardon?

DAVID: You know my views.

JEFF: I didn't.

ERIC: You see, Jeff didn't. Is this going to break up a potential relationship?

DAVID: They've never done anything for me.

ERIC: *(To JEFF.)* He did tell you he was an underpaid male nurse?

JEFF: No, he didn't.

ERIC: Well, he was.

JEFF: And being manager of a fast-food restaurant?

ERIC: He is - now.

DAVID: I am now because I couldn't afford to be a nurse.

ERIC: Not strictly true. You got sick of all the death and the dying. You can't blame the Tories for that. *(Turns to JEFF.)* One night he had to cope almost single handed on a geriatric ward, and this ancient woman had the nerve to go and die all over him. *(To DAVID.)* Do you remember how angry you were about that, David? You had dressed in your outdoor clothes - all ready to rush off to the latest disco - and she vomited blood all over them. How you bitched when you got back in all that soiled denim. *(Pause.)* He never forgave the NHS after that.

DAVID: *(Furious. Gets coat. To JEFF.)* We'd better get ready to leave.

ERIC: Going out?

JEFF: A party.

ERIC: Where?

JEFF: My office.

ERIC: Can you take him? I mean if you are in the closet he might drag you out.

JEFF: There is nothing wrong in taking a friend. Someone's birthday. There will be lots of her friends there.

ERIC: *(Slightly petulantly.)* Well, I'll just have to watch television alone, won't I? There's yet another programme about you know what. According to the blurb about this one there is a decrease in gays infecting each other. I wonder if they will show us as a shining example for the rest of the community?

DAVID: Some of us are.

ERIC: The truth is they have brain washed us into being too terrified to go near each other. Every time I see someone deep kissing I feel they are spreading germs. *(Laughs.)* It's a gut reaction now. Anyway, you two go and have fun. *(Turns to JEFF.)* Is it true you don't kiss at all?

(DAVID and JEFF exit without a word.)

(Stage darkens to denote the passing of time. Spotlight on ERIC.)

ERIC: *(Talking to an invisible DAVID.)* You don't like cats. You don't like cats so much it's an obsession, and now you are going to put our friendship aside for a man with a neutered tom. *(Pause.)* Let me tell you a story. *(Pause.)* No, listen. You'll never know if I made it up, but here goes. I had to go and see this couple. Both worried wells. With phantom Aids. Aids with all the symptoms that aren't medically real. Weight loss, sweating, panic, the lot. *(Pause.)* They asked me to come to their place. Lilac walls and pink curtains. I was given Earl Grey tea in thirties china. I listened, and they talked, and they were so pleased with what I didn't say they asked me to see their baby. *(Pause.)* It seems that Buster - the stereotyped butch lover - had bought his friend Bobby a baby toy cat to keep him company while he was at work. Bobby proudly went into the bedroom and brought out baby. *(Pause.)* Have you ever seen a toy cat on wheels? It was life size I guess - I mean in cat dimensions - and Bobby said Buster had got it reduced in a Hamley's sale. *(Pause.)* Cabaret time began. Bobby gave one clap of his hands, and Frisky, the toy cat, came forward, wheels charging. Then Bobby gave two claps, and it turned left, three claps followed and it turned right, and with four it whizzed backwards. Boring? *(Pause.)* It was boring. Then Bobby had the brilliant idea of putting music on. Ravel's "Bolero". It danced round in a circle, totally out of time to the music, and I got a headache with the sodding

Ravel. But oh no, cabaret time was not over. Bobby then showed me how if he stroked it at the back of its control panel it would purr at him - but somehow as much as he tried that dead toy moggy didn't have a shred of personality. Then he showed me how if you lock it in a certain mode it goes round exploring the room, meowing and purring. It could also get angry and thoughtful too. He showed me how when it's thoughtful it marches up and down. *(Pause.)* I'm not sure what it does when it's angry. He didn't show me that. Then he picked it up and it purred at him, opened it's big artificial cat eyes, flashed and fluttered them - and then grinned from ear to ear like the cat in "Alice in Wonderland". He called it his very own Frisky Baby Buster, and then he accidentally dropped it and one of its wheels came undone in the excitement. *(Long pause.)* All I could think of was how I wished it was real so it could piss on the lilac curtains. *(Longer pause.)* No, David, there is no point to this story. But it is no less boring David, than you being serious about spending your time with this bore Jeff, who puts his hands up computers. *(Quietly.)* I could make you happier than him.

BLACKOUT

SCENE SIX

(JEFF's flat. JEFF comes into the room first. DAVID follows a little out of breath.)

DAVID: *(Looking out of the window.)* Panoramic. I can see the Canary Wharf Tower. Just like New York.

JEFF: *(Proudly.)* The Docks.

DAVID: Must be expensive living here. *(Slight pause.)*
            We shouldn't be talking about money.

JEFF: There's nothing to be ashamed of in talking
            about money. I can afford it. *(Pause.)* That
            wasn't meant to impress.

DAVID: *(Goes to JEFF's stereo system and puts on a
            CD of "Phantom Of The Opera".)* I like being
            impressed. The last time I was impressed, and
            not bored with being impressed, I was sixteen.
            This guy took me out in his sports car. I had
            rather vulgar taste then. *(Turns to JEFF.)* You
            like this music? I didn't ask if I could put it on.

JEFF: It's alright.

DAVID: You're a fan?

JEFF: *(Awkwardly.)* I do like other music.

DAVID: Such as?

JEFF: Mostly singers. Barbara Cook. Eartha Kitt.
            (Pause.) I met Eartha Kitt at a party.

DAVID: I saw "Phantom of the Opera" and this woman
            in the audience screamed when the chandelier
            fell down.

(Long silence. JEFF turns off music.)

JEFF: I've got lots of photo albums. Do you like
            looking at photos?

DAVID: Of you?

JEFF: Me and my family. The group at work,
            including Tina who you met that night and
            liked.

DAVID: It would be fun to look at them.

JEFF: Afterwards I'll get us something to eat. It's cold
           I'm afraid. Marks and Spencer's chicken with
           salad. Not exactly a meal for a winter's night,
           but we could have it with lots of coffee.

DAVID: Sounds romantic.

JEFF: Now you're laughing at me. I'm sorry if I can't
           cook.

DAVID: Why should you? I can't either.

JEFF: I've come to depend upon Marks and Spencer's.

DAVID: I'll learn to cook and experiment on you.

*(They look at each other. JEFF moves towards DAVID as
if he wants to hold him. DAVID looks as if he is waiting for
this, then JEFF moves back.)*

JEFF: So you would like to see the photos?

DAVID: I want to see some baby ones of you. I haven't
           seen you naked yet.

*(JEFF sits beside DAVID on the floor. Suddenly he kisses
DAVID on the cheek. DAVID looks surprised, but neither
of them say anything. JEFF opens an album.)*

DAVID: Anyone I know here?

JEFF: *(Looks at him quizzically.)*

DAVID: A joke.

JEFF: *(Points to the fist photo.)* Me at four. That's
           Mum holding me. Dad's the fuzzy shadow in
           the background.

DAVID: Aren't they always? Fathers. Mine was fuzzy in
           the foreground.

JEFF: I love my father.

DAVID: I hate mine.

JEFF: *(Points to another photo.)* Mum again. And that's my sister Pauline. Pauline was a nurse.

DAVID: Is that a reminder?

JEFF: She had potential.

DAVID: I'm sure.

JEFF: But she became a mother, and anyway her husband always supplemented her nurse's income. It was pin money for her what she earned. *(Pause.)* Best the way it is now, her at home, although I admired her for having a vocation. *(Pause.)* Despite what Eric says it was a vocation for you too wasn't it?

DAVID: *(Sarcastically.)* A passion.

JEFF: I'm far too selfish for that kind of passion.

DAVID: *(Impatiently.)* I didn't mean that to be taken seriously. Shall we move on with the photos? *(Pause.)* I want to see your ex-lovers.

JEFF: I've only had one. Remember?

DAVID: *(Pointing to the album.)* Is he here?

JEFF: I'm not sure I want to point him out. You might be critical.

DAVID: On the other hand he might make me feel inferior. *(Pause.)* Please, I'm dying of curiosity. *(Pause.)* Who's the rather plump looking young man -

JEFF: Guess?

DAVID: Can't. It's fuzzy again. Someone you knew couldn't take photos.

JEFF: It's me.

DAVID: You!

JEFF: I was eighteen.

DAVID: But you had a moustache!

JEFF: I had a moustache. *(Pause.)* I wasn't the best looking teenager in Surbiton. That's where we lived.

DAVID: You've changed.

JEFF: Look, this was a lousy idea about the photos. We could be here for ages.

DAVID: I've got ages.

JEFF: We could be doing more interesting things.

DAVID: We could, but you'd accuse me of having a one track mind again. *(Pause.)* What I want to know is, how does a plump, rather unassuming teenager turn into a yummy, well-dressed yuppie who is into computers?

JEFF: *(Looks.)*

DAVID: *(Picking up the album.)* I'll just flick through and find that man who was in your life.

JEFF: *(Embarrassed.)* Don't -

DAVID: *(Laughing.)* So he wasn't attractive? *(Pause.)* I'm always teasing you aren't I? Why don't you play some music while we look? Like Barbra Streisand singing opera. Or Barbara Cook.

JEFF: *(Takes the photo album from him.)* We could watch television.

DAVID: Isn't that the last resort for the unimaginative?

(Long pause.)

JEFF: Well, I've got a confession to make.

DAVID: *(Brightly.)* You have? Porno movies?

JEFF: Please...

DAVID: Sorry.

JEFF: Playing games. I've done some practising.

DAVID: *(Suspiciously.)* Who with?

JEFF: Tina at work.

DAVID: So what have you learnt?

JEFF: Practically all the literary questions in the
           Trivial Pursuits boxes. *(Pause.)* Plus the
           answers.

DAVID: I can believe you did do that.

JEFF: I'm a Capricorn. I'm tenacious and ambitious,
           and I learn quickly.

DAVID: Don't be ridiculous, you can't be serious about
           star signs. *(Pause.)* So you want us to try out
           having a game now?

JEFF: It's good for awkward moments.

DAVID: This being one?

JEFF: Not exactly.

DAVID: I think it is. You think it is. *(Pause.)* OK. Get
           out the board and the boxes.

(JEFF gets up and moves away to get the boxes.)

DAVID: *(Aside.)* Now he's learnt Trivial Pursuit
           questions and answers by heart we will never
           have sex.

BLACKOUT

SCENE SEVEN

*(ERIC and DAVID's flat. Evening. ERIC alone on stage.
DAVID enters, humming to himself.)*

ERIC: What's that awful tune?

DAVID: From a Sondheim musical.

ERIC: A what?

DAVID: A Sondheim musical.

ERIC: You don't like musicals.

DAVID: Amazing what you can get used to. It's catchy.
          Should give tunes a try.

ERIC: I don't like tunes.

DAVID: Sorry. Forgetting you're a modern opera queen.

ERIC: I like string quartets. *(Pause.)* By the way, he
          rang. He's had trouble with his computers. He
          sounded as if he was speaking from far away.
          Could he have left the country?

DAVID: Very funny.

ERIC: Not really. It's not really funny at all, seeing
          you making a spectacle of yourself humming
          Sondheim.

DAVID: Did he say anything else when he rang?

ERIC: No.

(Long pause.)

DAVID: I think I'm falling in love with him.

ERIC: Have you slept with him?

DAVID: What a question!

ERIC: A good one.

DAVID: He's celibate too.

ERIC: Interesting. All that sexual energy charged up
          between you and doing nothing. Not surprising
          you're listening to appalling music. It must
          make a nice background to all that mental
          wanking that's going on.

DAVID: Shut up, Eric.

ERIC: Touch home that one?

DAVID: You always touch home. *(Pause.)* I'm going
          upstairs to try and have another wank.

ERIC: You never were much good solo. Why don't
          you accept it and take up prayer beads instead?

DAVID: Praying is not my style. I'm a born again
          atheist. Unlike you -

ERIC: I don't believe.

DAVID: A repressed Catholic who had his first sexual
          experience hiding under an old priest's cassock
          will always believe.

ERIC: I want to watch television. *(Pause. Long look at
          DAVID. Tentatively.)* Will you stay in tonight?

DAVID: Do you want me to?

ERIC: Have you anything else better to do? I mean
          have you a night off from expensive bad taste in
          the Docklands? Because if you have anything
          else better -

DAVID: I don't have. Not really. *(Pause.)* Let's have a
          laugh tonight. Anything funny on telly?

ERIC: We'll make the jokes if there isn't.

DAVID: Don't we always?

*(Long pause. They look affectionately at each other.
DAVID breaks the mood.)*

DAVID: By the way next week Jeff's coming round with
          a friend.

BLACKOUT

SCENE EIGHT

(ERIC and DAVID's flat. Evening. ERIC, DAVID and JEFF waiting in a pastiche position recalling Chekhov's "Three Sisters". ERIC is gazing into space. DAVID is seated. JEFF standing a little away from them.)

ERIC: *(Pure theatre.)* Oh, Moscow, Moscow... why are we waiting? *(Pause.)* That lovely city on the Neva.

JEFF: That's Leningrad.

ERIC: How clever of you to know about St. Petersburg. *(Pause.)* Why are we waiting? *(Turns to JEFF.)* Can you tell me?

JEFF: He must have got held up in the traffic.

ERIC: But Jeff, you told him to meet us here at seven. It's gone eight.

DAVID: Maybe he changed his mind about coming.

ERIC: Teachers do not change their minds. The one mind that they do have usually stays firmly in one place. *(Pause.)* Where did you say he teaches, Jeff?

JEFF: Ealing.

ERIC: How nice. Is he good-looking? Will I like him?

JEFF: He's had problems. You know that.

ERIC: Has that affected his looks?

DAVID: Eric, don't be superficial.

JEFF: *(Aside.)* Or not more than you really are.

ERIC: I may be flippant, but I am not superficial. I am also getting hungry, and all the restaurants will be taking last orders at this rate.

DAVID: There's always somewhere open.

ERIC: Yes, but I don't want to go to Earls Court.

JEFF: We will find somewhere.

ERIC: The restaurants I have in mind book out early.

DAVID: Then why didn't you book?

ERIC: He may not be able to afford my kind of restaurant. It's manners to ask first. *(To JEFF.)* You obviously did not think of that.

JEFF: I'll ring. *(Picks up phone, dials. Silence while the three wait for an answer. No reply.)* Not in. That's a good sign.

ERIC: He doesn't have an answering machine?

(Doorbell.)

ERIC: That must be him. I'll go and put on some cologne.

DAVID: Don't be ridiculous. A depressed teacher is hardly going to be your sort.

ERIC: I'm always ready to impress.

JEFF: Eric, you are not a camp person, not really, so why play up now when I want you to be serious?

ERIC: I will put on my counselling smile, and wear my heart on my sleeve.

(JEFF exits and immediately returns, followed by KEITH. He is very quiet looking and is dressed in jeans and a badly fitting jacket.)

ERIC: *(Moving forward.)* You must be Keith.

KEITH: Yes.

ERIC: I'm Eric. *(Pointing to DAVID.)* This is David, my long-suffering flat-sharer.

DAVID: Friends actually. *(Shakes Keith's hand.)* Pleased to meet you, Keith. Jeff has mentioned you quite a lot.

ERIC: *(Sarcastically.)* Has he?

KEITH: I'm sure he couldn't have had anything very interesting to say.

ERIC: Do I notice a touch of Scotland in your accent?

KEITH: I went to Stirling University, then I taught in Oban.

DAVID: Oh, that's very interesting.

ERIC: Very!

DAVID: *(Covering for ERIC's rudeness.)* I went there when I was a child. A week's holiday. I remember being seasick on the ferry over to Mull.

KEITH: Mull's not very exciting.

DAVID: Well, it rather depends what you like. Personally -

ERIC: *(Interrupting.)* Personally David likes looking at men, Keith. Men in groups and lots of them - so it would not have been a place he would have liked. *(General embarrassment at this.)* Actually Keith, David is used to the wide open spaces. He was born on a farm, so there would have been some rapport with Mull.

DAVID: I was not born on a farm.

KEITH: *(Laughs nervously.)* I'd rather not talk about Scotland. I got away from the place so as to never have to do that again.

ERIC: I like the Scots.

DAVID: *(Looks at ERIC.)* Especially if they pump oil and come from Aberdeen. *(Turns to Keith.)* What will you have, Keith? There is -

ERIC: A vodka household mainly, but we do have some gin and I think we have scotch.

KEITH: A lager would be fine.

ERIC: *(To DAVID.)* Do we have any lager? *(Pause.)* As we are going out I thought it might not be the sort of aperitif you'd like. *(Aside to DAVID.)* I can't imagine anyone drinking lager before a meal.

KEITH: Oh, I drink anything really.

JEFF: You still want to go out for a meal, Keith?

KEITH: Yes, but I'm a bit poor at the moment. Not like you Jeff. Rich in computers.

ERIC: We haven't seen any of his money. He's so nicely shy with it. Are you shy, Keith?

KEITH: Sorry. Shy where?

ERIC: Anywhere. In general.

KEITH: Like everyone else I have my moments.

ERIC: I bet you're not shy in the classroom.

KEITH: Well, that's where you are wrong. Sometimes I clam up and just make them do exercises. So as not to talk to them. *(Longer pause.)* Like today.

ERIC: Why today? Panic at meeting us?

KEITH: I'd rather not talk about it.

ERIC: I understand. Don't be intimidated by us. I can be a bit overbearing, but I am assured I am the sort of person you can get used to. Ask Jeff.

JEFF: I'll vouch for that.

DAVID: Don't believe that lie.

ERIC: That's what I love about certain friends Keith,
           how supportive they can be - even with our lies.
           (To DAVID.) Get Jeff and I a drink. You know
           what we want.

DAVID: *(Coldly.)* I'm just the maid here.

ERIC: *(To JEFF.)* With ice? The drink?

JEFF: No ice for me.

ERIC: *(Turns to DAVID.)* No ice for Jeff. *(DAVID
           exits. ERIC turns to KEITH.)* How long have
           you known Jeff? We've only had the pleasure of
           his company for a short while.

KEITH: *(Looks at JEFF.)* Shall I...?

JEFF: Yes. Go ahead.

ERIC: This sounds like a secret. Lovers? *(Pause.)*
           Were you lovers?

KEITH: Oh no, we met at a straight party. We told each
           other we were gay under the effect of alcohol,
           then went our separate ways. We both felt out
           of place there, which made it easy to confide in
           each other. To be honest I did fancy him.
           (Pause.) Then we bumped into each other a
           couple of months later, and we've been friends
           ever since.

ERIC: What a nice story.

JEFF: A bit banal.

ERIC: Most best stories are. Sometimes banal things
           sustain the interest more than complicated
           things. *(To JEFF.)* I am sure David would agree
           about that, wouldn't you Jeff?

KEITH: That's a bit too profound for me.

ERIC: What, for an intelligent school teacher?

KEITH: I'm not very bright. I just teach my subject
           moderately well.

(DAVID returns with the drinks.)

DAVID: *(Handing JEFF and ERIC their drinks.)* What
           do you teach?

KEITH: Maths.

DAVID: Oh.

JEFF: He's good at it too. *(To KEITH.)* You've helped
           me out of a few mathematical problems, haven't
           you, Keith?

KEITH: If you say so.

DAVID: I thought computers was all mathematics.

ERIC: *(To JEFF.)* Ah, but what have you helped Keith
           with?

JEFF: *(Evasively.)* I help.

DAVID: Well, at least the subject of homosexuality
           doesn't crop up in maths. No danger of you
           having to come out in the class on that subject.
           Not like literature with all those risky authors.

ERIC: Since when did you read a book?

DAVID: I read.

JEFF: *(To KEITH.)* These two seem to spend their
           time knocking sparks off each other.

ERIC: What awful boy scout imagery. *(Observing
           KEITH.)* Aren't we rude? We've completely
           forgotten your lager.

JEFF: *(Immediately.)* I'll get you one.

(JEFF leaves the room.)

KEITH: *(After a long pause.)* Jeff told me that you are a counsellor, Eric.

ERIC: Naughty Jeff.

KEITH: Oh, he didn't mean to gossip. It's just that -

ERIC: If you make me talk about my job I'll have you tell us how you solve all those awful equations. I'm sure you wouldn't like that.

KEITH: But what you do isn't boring.

ERIC: I'm sure Einstein didn't find maths boring, except those around him must have yawned their way into relativity.

DAVID: *(Tactfully.)* I think Keith may have a specific reason for asking.

ERIC: Oh. Do you, Keith?

(JEFF returns with KEITH's drink. ERIC turns to JEFF.)

ERIC: Jeff, why did you tell Keith what I did for a living?

JEFF: Keith asked. If I did wrong -

DAVID: Of course you weren't wrong Jeff. You've just taken Eric's mysterious aura away from him, that's all.

(KEITH drops his lager. It spills into the carpet. ERIC lets out a loud "Oh". KEITH bends down and starts wiping at the stain with a handkerchief.)

KEITH: *(Almost in tears.)* Sorry.

DAVID: It's not important. It's an old carpet that should have been ripped up and chucked out a long time ago.

ERIC: Yes, it came with the flat. Don't worry about it.
             Any new stain just makes it more urgent to
             change it.

*(KEITH bursts into tears. ERIC and JEFF look on in
silence. Neither of them know what to do. JEFF looks
surprised and ERIC a bit appalled. DAVID looks away.)*

ERIC: *(After a long pause. Coldly.)* Is anything
             wrong?

KEITH: *(Straightens up.)* I shouldn't have come here.

JEFF: Don't be daft, Keith. I asked you. I wanted my
             new friends to meet you.

KEITH: It wasn't the right day.

ERIC: *(Stupidly.)* Did we mix our days?

JEFF: *(Turns on ERIC.)* Don't be smart, Eric. You can
             see he's distressed.

KEITH: I shouldn't have come.

ERIC: Please don't keep on saying that and standing.
             Sit down.

DAVID: I could make some tea.

ERIC: Tea, Keith?

KEITH: *(Sitting.)* I'll be alright.

*(Long awkward silence. ERIC, DAVID and JEFF are
standing behind KEITH. ERIC looks at DAVID who shrugs
his shoulders. JEFF turns away. The silence continues.
KEITH stares into space, then suddenly cries out like a
wounded animal. All three behind him start, looking at
each other in panic.)*

KEITH: *(Blurting it out in a rush.)* My lover died of
             Aids, and now -today I got the result for myself
             from the clinic. I'm HIV positive.

(Silence.)

KEITH: Mark, my lover, he died in such distress. He
was covered with those bloody purple things.
Kaposi's. I thought people with Aids didn't get
Kaposi's anymore, but Mark did. On his face,
in his groin. Inside his body making him yell
with pain. *(Pause.)* I couldn't cope. I said to him
in the hospital, "I can't cope with seeing you
deteriorate like this." I was scared to touch him.
I only kissed him at the end when he was dead,
and lying there dead. I couldn't kiss him while
he was living. *(Long pause.)* You don't know
what it's like to witness things about your lover
that were private, and that suddenly are no
longer. Watching as he is held as he goes to the
bath because he can't manage on his own.
Watching how he is washed after he has soiled
the bed and how everything on the bed must be
changed. *(Pause.)* When you are young and
attractive and waiting around in clubs and bars
you don't think this could happen to you. *(Long
silence. KEITH wearily rubs his face with his
hands, then begins to speak again.)* One night
we went out for a meal. He was too tired to
cook at home, and he said it might do him good
to eat out. *(Pause.)* The only place open near us
was a small caff where they do steak and
kidney pie, fish and chips, that sort of thing. He
couldn't eat it all, and in the middle of eating he
got a coughing attack. A bad one. We got out
into the street. It was cold, and the coughing got
worse. I thought he was about to collapse, the
effort was so great to keep going with that
cough. *(Pause.)* Then he doubled over, and
there - there in the gutter, he vomited up the
little of the fish and chips he had eaten, and his
body eventually straightened up and he looked

so worn out with the pain of that cough - and I knew as I looked at him that it would go on like this, the small indignities perhaps greater than the pain - and worse, that I too, selfishly felt sorry for myself because I was lost and alone with it. *(Pause.)* I didn't know what to do. Supposing a Policeman had seen him. I could imagine Mark saying, because he was bloody brave - "No, I'm not drunk, Officer, I've got Aids." *(Pause.)* Fear is fear.

ERIC: I'm sure you did everything you could. You mustn't give yourself such a rough time now.

KEITH: Bollocks. I was scared for myself. *(To ERIC.)* Do you know what it's like?

ERIC: *(Defensively.)* Personally?

KEITH: Yes.

ERIC: I've counselled people with Aids. I have been there.

KEITH: Where? Not there. Not in the bed.

ERIC: How could I be? I'm -

KEITH: Not sick!

ERIC: Not to my knowledge.

JEFF: Keith, this is not helping.

KEITH: I didn't cry at the clinic when they told me. I should have cried there today. They asked if they could counsel me then.

ERIC: Maybe you should have let them.

KEITH: *(Screams out.)* I didn't need it then.

JEFF: Don't.

KEITH: *(Suddenly quiet.)*

DAVID: I'll make some tea.

JEFF: No, I'll make the tea.

DAVID: Really, Jeff, I know where everything is.

JEFF: I know the kitchen as well.

DAVID: I would like to make the tea.

(This last exchange between DAVID and JEFF should be played in a panic comedy style. In some ways the "comedy" in the play ends here. Both JEFF and DAVID exit.)

KEITH: They say it's good for shock.

ERIC: After the tea Keith, I suggest you get Jeff to take you home, and then you can have a talk with him.

KEITH: *(Dully.)* Yes. *(Long pause.)* Why does it happen?

ERIC: What?

KEITH: The death. The loss.

ERIC: It happens.

KEITH: Do you get hardened to this? *(Pause.)* People like me?

ERIC: I hope I don't.

KEITH: Are you feeling anything now? While you're watching me? I want you to be honest with me.

ERIC: I can see you're going through a bad time.

KEITH: No, I mean you. Do you feel anything?

ERIC: It's not my problem, is it? *(Pause.)* It's not happening to me.

KEITH: So, I'm a case? A non-allocated case?

ERIC: You are a friend's friend. *(Pause.)* I'm sorry your lover died, and that you had the news you had today. *(Pause.)* Don't you believe me?

KEITH: I'm sorry too, but I don't believe you.

ERIC: I think you are in shock.

KEITH: Don't you ever say the word "feel"?

ERIC: Isn't this rather playing with words?

KEITH: Do I look as if I'm bloody playing with words?

ERIC: I think you should get help from the counsellor you saw this morning. He or she -

KEITH: She.

ERIC: She must know all about it.

KEITH: All about it? You mean about the panic inside me? The memory of Mark in the street and of him struggling in bed for his life?

ERIC: I don't mean that.

KEITH: What do you mean then?

ERIC: *(Turns away.)* I don't know.

KEITH: Chances are I will die too, won't I?

ERIC: That's not what you must think.

KEITH: *(Shouts.)* Feel. Feel!

ERIC: *(Shouts back.)* All right then. Feel!

(Long silence.)

KEITH: *(Slowly.)* Do you find me attractive?

ERIC: *(Forces an embarrassed laugh.)* What?

KEITH: Do you find me attractive?

ERIC: No one is attractive when they are in shock.

KEITH: *(Shouts.)* Do you find me attractive?

ERIC: No.

KEITH: Would you be more sympathetic if you did?

BLACKOUT

SCENE NINE

(ERIC and DAVID's flat. About an hour later. DAVID and JEFF are seated side by side. ERIC is standing at a distance from them.)

JEFF: I shouldn't have let him go off on his own.

DAVID: That's what he wanted.

JEFF: That's what he said he wanted.

ERIC: He didn't want you with him. He wanted to be on his own.

JEFF: I failed him.

ERIC: Don't be silly. You can't force people, or go against their wishes.

JEFF: He was in such a state.

ERIC: He was calm when he left. There is only so much one can do.

JEFF: And we did it?

ERIC: That's sounds like a question, but I will take it as a statement. We did it.

JEFF: Did what? Made Tea? Both of you would have packed him a take away dinner if you could have. *(Pause.)* You both couldn't wait to get him out of here because he opened up his wounds.

ERIC: Jeff, I wasn't in a dressing wounds mood. I've had a hard day, and I like to come home to relax.

JEFF: And he was work?

ERIC: In a way, yes. He is your friend, not ours.

DAVID: That's unfair.

JEFF: *(Avoiding this.)* He's suffering.

ERIC: Being in computers, or calculations, or whatever the dreary work it is that you do, you may have missed out on the fact that the whole fucking world is suffering. *(Pause.)* But fortunately a lot of people are reticent about showing it.

DAVID: It was unexpected.

JEFF: But it happened. And we weren't there for him. Not really.

ERIC: What is this suddenly - a court of law? The last judgement?

JEFF: How cold you are.

DAVID: Eric is tired.

JEFF: And cold. *(Pause.)* How did you get into counselling?

ERIC: I'm finding this insulting.

DAVID: Jeff, we did do in our way what we could.

ERIC: I got into counselling by being practical. By taking a few steps backwards and looking at a situation. At the moment I suggest that you do the same.

JEFF: Another way of saying not getting really involved?

ERIC: Is it? So what would you suggest? Total
            immersion into the problems that people with
            HIV are having? Identification? Is that it? That
            would be a great help. It would be suffocating,
            patronising, and would also mean being a bad
            professional. You can't, can't be in another
            person's place, or show them that you identify
            too much.

JEFF: *(Shouting too.)* Cop out and you know it.

DAVID: Stop.

JEFF: It is. You don't care enough.

ERIC: *(Coldly.)* And you do?

JEFF: Yes.

ERIC: In what way have you cared about Keith?

JEFF: He's one of my best friends.

ERIC: Best?

JEFF: He rings me, I call round. I ring him, call round.

ERIC: Sounds casual Jeff. Hardly committed. Were
            you there - even in the background - when his
            lover was dying?

JEFF: But -

ERIC: Were you in the waiting room at the hospital?
            Did you run to him then?

JEFF: No.

ERIC: Why?

JEFF: He didn't ask.

ERIC: But you knew what a state he'd be in. You must
            have realised you don't - as a friend - wait
            around to be asked? It's basic to run to friends
            in need. *(Pause.)* You see that is the difference -

	counsellors do not run. We are asked. Friends impose, counsellors don't.
DAVID:	This is getting us nowhere.
ERIC:	I didn't have to do anything. I am not at work. He is not my case. He is not my friend. I don't wish to discuss this further.
JEFF:	It seems to me that out of office hours a person with Aids needs to look like Tom Cruise.
ERIC:	That's cheap.
JEFF:	Is it? *(Pause.)* How much do we stick to our own kind? Even in extremis? Good looks, cars, good money? *(To DAVID.)* Would you have wanted me if I had been that dumpy teenager in the photo?
DAVID:	I don't like teenagers.
JEFF:	You know what I mean.
ERIC:	Lucky David if he does, I certainly don't.
JEFF:	I failed him. I admit it. If I hadn't known him for years maybe I wouldn't want to get too close - I mean he's not the kind I go around with. Boring - to me - but someone in need, and he needs my friendship. *(Pause.)* I didn't do my best.
DAVID:	Then why should you expect us to do better?
JEFF:	Because people like you are supposed to care.
DAVID:	I run a fast food restaurant, remember?
ERIC:	*(Laughs.)*
JEFF:	You were a nurse.

ERIC: I don't weep, Jeff, for people I don't know. The little best that I have in me is rationed. Bit like a war effort really.

JEFF: Poor Eric.

ERIC: I return the compliment. Poor Jeff. *(Kisses JEFF scornfully on the mouth.)*

JEFF: *(Pulls away. Shouts.)* Bastards. Self-centred, egotistical bastards. That's what Aids has made us become.

ERIC: That's what we always were.

(Silence.)

JEFF: I said I failed.

ERIC: Noble words. But you Jeff are nervous around Aids. You said so yourself.

JEFF: So?

ERIC: So. So am I. I'm nervous. Scared too. Have you thought of that? And yes, I'm cold too. I laugh at a lot of things I perhaps shouldn't laugh at - but who is to say you can't die on a good laugh? I'm not a walking gravestone just because I counsel people who in all probability are going to die.

JEFF: You're cold, and I'm feeling cold. I'll go to Keith.

ERIC: Good. *(Half singing.)* Bye!

JEFF: Won't be around for a while.

DAVID: *(Coldly.)* Is that what you want?

JEFF: Something essential to say at last?

DAVID: I was listening.

JEFF: I suppose you agree with him?

DAVID: I live with Eric. I share his laughs. *(Pause.)* Do you want me to come with you?

JEFF: It might not be humorous enough for you. *(Pause.)* Anyway Eric needs you. It's funny how two humorous guys like you can be too bloody serious for me.

ERIC: Jeff, two points before you go. Point one - I do so hate to be serious at home. Point two -you have absolutely no sense of humour.

BLACKOUT

SCENE TEN

(JEFF's flat. Evening. KEITH is alone on stage. He is standing, obviously waiting for JEFF to return. He paces the room for a while, then sits down and begins to hug himself. He starts as he hears the key go in the lock. JEFF enters.)

JEFF: *(Cautiously.)* You alright?

KEITH: *(Laughs.)* You always ask me that. You've taken away all the knives that cut, you've got no pills in the flat, and I'm scared of heights. *(Pause.)* How could I commit suicide?

JEFF: Walk out of the door.

KEITH: And get run over by a bus?

JEFF: I meant you could walk out of the door and leave here. I'm not keeping you prisoner.

KEITH: Maybe it keeps me going feeling you are keeping me prisoner. *(Pause.)* Had a good day?

JEFF: *(Nods his head.)*

KEITH: Now I sound like a housewife. An opposite role really. Mark used to ask me that.

JEFF: *(Sits down, stares into space. It's obvious he doesn't want to talk.)*

KEITH: Every time you come back I want to tell you how grateful I am that you talked me into coming here. I don't know what I would have -

JEFF: Every time I come back you do tell me how grateful you are. *(Curtly.)* For once don't.

KEITH: I don't have to - it's not gratitude. I made a decision today. Don't look so surprised. I can make decisions.

JEFF: I've never doubted that. You came here -

KEITH: Precisely.

JEFF: Well?

KEITH: Precisely that. I made the decision to come here, so I must make the decision to go. *(JEFF wants to speak but KEITH silences him.)* No, listen to me. I've recovered here. I've read a lot and not thought a great deal. I've turned your tidy flat into a bookshop when it's never seen a book, and I've generally emptied my mind of - well, of everything. I've also loved not going anywhere; of not having to make dinner in case you thought I'd try the tin opener on my wrists as the knives are so blunt. I've had a holiday, Jeff. I haven't thought of maths, or children, or that bloody school that always stays open longer than anywhere else at holiday time. I've even liked the view of the docks, and imagined I was rich.

JEFF: *(Slowly.)* I am not rich.

KEITH: I know you're not. I know too you have been - generous.

JEFF: I wanted to do it.

KEITH: I'm not putting that into question, but I can also sense that it is time for me to go back - *(Long pause.)* - home.

JEFF: Mark's house?

KEITH: Our house. Makes it more of a challenge to plunge in at the deep end. *(Pause.)* If I get depressed I can always come back here, can't I?

(JEFF opens two cans of lager from a shopping bag.)

KEITH: That's another thing I've noticed -

JEFF: What?

KEITH: Since I've been here you drink out of cans. A month of this and you'll be as much of a slob as I am.

JEFF: Don't put yourself down.

KEITH: I'm not. It's just I'd better get back to mixing with people on my own level.

JEFF: *(Offended.)* Thanks.

KEITH: No offence, but I don't fit here, Jeff. How many people have you had back since I've been here?

JEFF: I don't know that many people. I'm a loner, remember?

KEITH: Even the cat behaves as if it's a pedigree.

JEFF: It's a moggy.

KEITH: Then why do you always buy it "Sheba" and not ordinary cat food? When we, Mark and I had a cat, we never fed it "Sheba". *(Pause.)* Mark says - *(Stops, realising what he is saying. Long pause. He begins again.)* Mark says he will never let any pet behave above its station. *(Pause.)* That word "station". Did you know Mark used to work for British Rail? He was

proud of going on strike when this country
believed in strikes.

(Silence.)

JEFF: Cry.

KEITH: *(Almost crying.)* Do you?

JEFF: Cry?

KEITH: Yes.

JEFF: Recently a lot.

KEITH: Missing him, aren't you?

JEFF: We don't have a thing in common.

KEITH: It's called love.

JEFF: It's also called stupidity.

KEITH: Ring him.

JEFF: No.

KEITH: Pride.

JEFF: Maybe.

KEITH: Pride's got a fall.

JEFF: I've had it. I'm immune to bruises. Let's change the subject.

KEITH: *(Quietly.)* Mark's joined this amateur dramatic company.

JEFF: *(Playing the game.)* Is he any good?

KEITH: They want him to play Hamlet. He calls it his Hamlet because he wants to play him as being gay. *(Slowly.)* One night when he was in hospital he wrote me a letter. *(Takes a pile of letters, scatters the letters on the floor.)* It must be here somewhere. *(Finds it.)* This one. *(Opens it, but doesn't read the words directly.)*

He asks me if he should do it - if he should perform in the play once he gets out. He's worried about the purple marks on his face.

JEFF: Easy, Keith.

KEITH: *(Quietly.)* It's not easy, it's not easy.

JEFF: *(Gently.)* I know.

KEITH: He says he wants to show them he can do it.

JEFF: I'm sure he - *(was going to say "could" but says)* - can.

KEITH: He was a good man. *(Pause.)* What am I talking about? I've no right to keep these letters. I wasn't there, not really there. I should have kissed those Kaposi's and told him he would be the best looking Hamlet ever.

JEFF: You are telling him that now.

KEITH: Am I?

JEFF: *(Bends down and picks up the scattered letters. Hands them to KEITH.)* Believe me.

KEITH: When I go home I'll talk to him some more.

JEFF: If that's what you want.

KEITH: It is. *(Pause.)* But I didn't tell you what he ends the letter with. He must have sensed the end was near. He finished the letter by writing, "Goodnight, sweet Prince." Do you know, I've never worked out if that was him saying goodbye to himself, or to me.

(JEFF reaches out and puts his hand on KEITH's shoulder.)

BLACKOUT

SCENE ELEVEN

(KEITH's house. Several weeks later. Stage slowly lightens. A single chair centre stage. A pile of books beside it. KEITH is seated on the chair, telephone in hand. He dials slowly, then stops. Begins to dial again. Raises the phone to his ear.)

KEITH: *(Long pause. He is listening to the ringing tone.)* Paul, it's Keith. Am I disturbing you? *(Pause.)* I intended to call. You were Mark's friend. *(Pause.)* Yes, thank you, I always felt welcome. *(Pause.)* Now? You mean, what am I doing now? *(Pause.)* Well, I'm here at home. There's a pile of stuff I want to read. That I need to read. *(Pause.)* What books? A mixed selection. Mark's books mainly. The ones I didn't read when he was - *(Long pause.)* It's alright. *(Pause.)* No, I'm not offended. Books help. They do for me anyway. "The Great Gatsby". Mark's favourite. I've never read it. I started to read it last night. *(Pause.)* Do you really want me to talk about the book? *(Forces a laugh.)* It's boring. The book's boring, and I feel guilty because I find it boring. *(Pause.)* Paul, I didn't ring you to discuss books. I wanted to - *(Pause.)* - yes, talk. I don't mind talking. *(Pause.)* No, I don't feel lonely. It's just I wanted to - *(Long pause.)* - talk. *(Pause.)* Yes, yes, I understand. Well, maybe we can meet up, perhaps here. You'll ring me? *(Pause.)* Dinner? *(Pause.)* I'll ring again...or you ring me. *(Pause.)* Now I feel awkward. It's just Mark thought a great deal of you, and...how's Ruth? Give her my - *(Slight pause.)* - best wishes. I know we only met once, but she seemed - *(Pause.)* - well, when she comes back. *(Pause.)*

Rome is nice. Mark went there. Sent me lots of
postcards. *(Pause.)* Yes. Goodbye.

*(Replaces receiver. Stares into space. Stage darkens to
denote the passage of time. Lightens again. KEITH is
pacing the room. The doorbell rings. He doesn't answer
immediately, but tidies up the books instead. The doorbell
rings again. He answers the door. JEFF walks in. They
stare at each other for a moment in silence. They both
speak at once.)*

KEITH: I wasn't expecting -

JEFF: I meant to come before.

KEITH: It's a surprise.

JEFF: I'm glad you're in.

(Long pause.)

KEITH: Would you like some coffee? Tea? I haven't got
          any alcohol.

JEFF: Nothing. I can't stop long.

KEITH: *(With a note of bitterness.)* It doesn't take long
          to drink tea.

JEFF: That's not what I meant.

KEITH: I know. *(Pause.)* I'm glad you came. *(Pause.)*
          The place is a mess. I haven't done the washing
          up for days. It all smells a bit doesn't it?

JEFF: I can't smell anything.

KEITH: I had onions for dinner. They stink the place
          out. I'll open some windows.

JEFF: Keith, please relax.

KEITH: I am relaxed. That's the trouble. Too relaxed.
          (Pause.) No one has been here.

JEFF: No one?

KEITH: *(Defensively.)* It's what I wanted.

JEFF: *(Short pause.)* I know.

KEITH: All the same it has been - lonely.

JEFF: I meant to come before.

KEITH: You've said that once.

JEFF: I mean it.

KEITH: *(Slight scorn.)* But you wanted to respect my privacy?

JEFF: Yes.

KEITH: In my situation people do tend to respect privacy. *(Looks hard at JEFF.)* It's called leaving people on their own.

JEFF: Other people. Not me.

KEITH: Yes, other people.

JEFF: *(Long pause.)* It's no good feeling bitter.

KEITH: What would you know?

JEFF: I just know.

KEITH: I don't think you do. *(Pause.)* I'm not bitter. And before you say it, it's not self-pity.

JEFF: I'm trying to see all this clearly.

KEITH: *(Laughs.)* The mess in the house? The mess in me? Clearly? You don't exactly need a microscope to find the flaws here - in the house - in me.

JEFF: Maybe you should return to that counsellor. The woman...

KEITH: *(Interrupting.)* Or your friend? *(Long pause.)* Sorry. That was unfair.

JEFF: Eric's breaking down under the strain of it all. I should have known when I took you there. *(Pause.)* When you came to stay I apologised for him if you remember.

KEITH: I remember. *(Pause.)* How is he?

JEFF: Okay I think.

KEITH: And his friend?

JEFF: I haven't rung yet, if that's what you're asking.

KEITH: I wasn't really asking. It's not my problem, is it? *(Pause.)* I can't listen to other people's problems. *(Slight pause.)* Not that I've had much risk of that recently. *(Slowly.)* Do you know how quiet it is talking to...? *(He stops.)*

JEFF: To Mark?

KEITH: *(Nods his head.)* It's so quiet doing that. I try to believe I hear replies, but I can't go on fooling myself. *(Long pause.)* I'll make some coffee.

JEFF: If you want.

(Neither of them move.)

JEFF: *(Slowly.)* What is it that you do want?

KEITH: *(Quietly.)* I want someone to touch me. I want someone to hold me. I want to kiss someone's lips again. *(Pause.)* Then I feel guilty because I'm thinking of someone else, and not Mark.

JEFF: It's normal -

KEITH: *(Quickly.)* To want someone? To want someone against your body, telling you it's alright, when it's not alright? *(Pause.)* I am not, I am not feeling sorry for myself. I'll go crazy if I blame myself for that as well. And then why shouldn't

	I feel sorry for myself? *(Shouts.)* The bed is cold.

JEFF: Yes. *(Pause.)* Mine too.

KEITH: I...

(Long pause.)

JEFF: Yes?

KEITH: Nothing.

JEFF: No, tell me.

KEITH: I was thinking of that party, when we first met. I was thinking that I -

JEFF: Go on.

KEITH: I can't say it.

JEFF: I want you to say it. That you desired me. That you still desire me. *(Pause.)* You want me to hold you, don't you? *(Pause.)* You must tell me.

KEITH: *(Shakes his head.)* You don't want me. It would be pity.

JEFF: Partly, yes.

KEITH: I don't want you to. Not out of pity.

JEFF: I said partly. The other part is, well I don't know how to put it - a closeness. *(Pause.)* Maybe we could be close sexually without pretence.

KEITH: Without love.

JEFF: With friendship.

KEITH: Ah, yes, friendship. Friendship took me round to your friend's place, didn't it?

JEFF: Not a friend.

KEITH: And I came away feeling I had been pissed on. *(Pause.)* If you held me, tonight in my bed, and then you left - and I felt humiliated - it would be the same. *(Long pause.)* I was cleaning out the attic a week ago. I found a pile of Mark's school things. Books mostly. I didn't even know they were there. I found an old nursery rhyme book - and a strange little book of animal humiliations. You know, animals dressed up as humans, and going through the sort of shit we go through. *(Pause.)* There was a picture of these three preening birds and what looked like some bloody ugly starling. Underneath was the caption -"Three peacocks meet a very common bird. What fun!"

(Long pause.)

JEFF: It wasn't like that.

KEITH: A book from the nineteenth century.

JEFF: Don't Keith. *(Pause.)* Don't go on with this terrible self-pity. Those birds in that picture, those preening birds as you called them - am I really that to you? Am I really the third bird in that picture? *(Pause.)* And what sort of an image do you have of yourself? You talking of being pissed on. Aren't you pissing on yourself? *(Pause.)* Why can't you have enough self-esteem to accept that part of me would like to hold you close all night, would like to give you something - or is that too much of a challenge to accept that I want to give?

(Long silence.)

KEITH: *(Slowly.)* I want to go to bed with you.

(Neither move.)

JEFF: I want to as well.

KEITH: Stay with me.

JEFF: I want to.

KEITH: *(After a long pause. Looks hard at JEFF.)* Do you?

BLACKOUT

SCENE TWELVE

(ERIC seated. Picks up a magazine. DAVID at a distance from him almost as if he were in another room. DAVID plays the tape message of the man from Aberdeen. He plays it twice. His face totally impassive as he does so. ERIC begins to rub his sex as the tape ends. DAVID finds his newspaper cuttings. ERIC masturbates and DAVID is "unaware" of what ERIC is doing. He cuts up newspaper articles. ERIC cries out and stops rubbing himself.)

ERIC: I can't.

DAVID: *(Without turning round.)* What?

ERIC: I can't - *(Pause.)* - come.

(Long silence.)

DAVID: *(Pointing to an article.)* It says here -

ERIC: *(Screams.)* Stop. Just don't - go on with it. I want it to stop.

(DAVID stares ahead. Puts down newspaper.)

ERIC: The three of us met today. You, me and Jeff. We went to the cinema. We talked - and now we can't talk.

DAVID: I wasn't sure if you wanted to talk about it.

ERIC: About you and Jeff? It had to be resolved, didn't it?

DAVID: *(Standing up. Faces him.)* Was it? Resolved?

(They stare a long time at each other in silence.)

ERIC: He's serious about you. If nothing else it was
         right for me to make peace with him because of
         that. *(Long pause.)* And we did. We faked
         peace. *(Pause.)* Have you ever thought how
         easy it is to fake peace between people? The
         smiles? The half lies, the half telling the truth?
         As fake as our sex - when we did.

DAVID: Not fake.

ERIC: Not true.

DAVID: We became celibates. Remember? That was
         fake. Fake celibacy. *(Goes to phone.)* Well, I
         don't want that anymore.

ERIC: What are you going to do?

DAVID: Ring Jeff.

ERIC: Not now. I don't want to hear you.

DAVID: *(Picks up phone. Dials. Pause.)* The answering
         machine again.

ERIC: *(Shouts.)* Stop.

DAVID: *(Talks into the phone.)* Jeff, it's David. Will you
         spend the weekend with me? I would like you
         to spend the weekend with me.

ERIC: *(Still shouting.)* David, I won't listen -

DAVID: I want to be with you, Jeff. I'll teach you more
         games. Fun games. *(Pause.)* I will try to make
         our relationship work. *(Puts down phone.)*

ERIC: Did you mean that?

DAVID: I want a lover.

ERIC: You've got a lover.

DAVID: *(Moves close to ERIC. Mockingly serious.)*
           You?

(ERIC turns away. Long silence.)

DAVID: *(Slowly.)* I know you love me.

ERIC: Don't say that.

DAVID: Why not?

ERIC: Because there is nothing I can say.

DAVID: I want you to.

ERIC: No way.

DAVID: Then tell me you really want me to go off with
           Jeff.

ERIC: Your decision.

DAVID: No, your turn to play. Your turn to make the
           move.

ERIC: I don't make moves.

DAVID: *(Quietly.)* Help me. Help me. *(Shouts.)* And if
           you can't help me, counsel me. You're good at
           that.

ERIC: *(As if playing.)* Are you dying? Are you ill? Are
           you a worried well?

DAVID: I'm scared.

ERIC: We are all scared. *(Pause.)* And there is no
           solution.

DAVID: There is. Tell me.

ERIC: *(In a sing-song voice.)* You've got me, you've
           got me, you've got me. *(Seriously.)* Do you
           honestly want me to say it?

(Long silence. They look at each other.)

ERIC: Will you fuck with him?

DAVID: Do you want me to fuck with him?

ERIC: Don't play games. Not anymore.

DAVID: I can only play games. It's all there is. Games.
          And these cuttings. *(Picks up a handful of
          cuttings and tears them to pieces.)* The
          scrapbooks.

ERIC: Is that a game too? The scrapbooks?

*(DAVID looks down at the torn cuttings at his feet. He
speaks slowly.)*

DAVID: Do you love me?

ERIC: I...

DAVID: *(Louder.)* Do you love me?

ERIC: *(Exhausted.)* I have nothing to give you.

DAVID: *(Shouts.)* Do you love me?

ERIC: I...

DAVID: *(Shouts louder.)* Do you?

ERIC: Yes.

(DAVID cries out. Silence.)

DAVID: Shut up.

BLACKOUT

END OF PLAY

THE ICE PICK

Characters

MICHAEL, in late twenties

PETER, more or less MICHAEL's age

MICHAEL's FATHER, in his fifties

ADAM, MICHAEL's closest friend

TIM, a doctor friend of PETER's

ERIC, a counsellor

MAN AT PARTY, probably in his thirties

Place

London, 1989

SCENE ONE

(An Aids Helpline. PETER is sorting through a pile of papers. MICHAEL enters. Unobserved by PETER he watches him in silence. He coughs slightly and moves forward. PETER looks up from the papers, startled, then smiles. MICHAEL moves towards him.)

MICHAEL: You're one of the party I haven't met.

PETER: *(Surprised.)* I -

MICHAEL: I'm Michael. *(Offers his hand.)*

PETER: I'm Peter. *(They shake hands.)*

MICHAEL: I've met most of the others. *(Pause.)* By the way, where's the toilet?

PETER: Next room.

MICHAEL: Hold on. Don't run away. I'll be back.

(MICHAEL rushes out. PETER gives a big sigh, clearly showing his pleasure at having met MICHAEL. MICHAEL re-enters, and looks at PETER for a moment again in silence.)

MICHAEL: The spread is excellent.

PETER: *(Laughs.)* The what?

MICHAEL: The spread. The food.

PETER: *(Smiles.)* Oh yes. Glad you like it.

MICHAEL: It's a change seeing vegetable dishes. None of this shoving dead animals down your throat.

PETER: Then you're a vegetarian?

MICHAEL: *(Laughs.)* I enjoy watching vegetarians. Gives me something to aspire to. *(Pause.)* Are you eating?

PETER: Well, I'm not -

MICHAEL: Vegetarian?

(PETER laughs awkwardly.)

MICHAEL: Have some food with me.

PETER: I've eaten already.

MICHAEL: With the group?

PETER: Before I came here.

MICHAEL: Didn't they tell you there was going to be food?

PETER: I knew there would be. I preferred eating at home.

MICHAEL: Then have a drink. *(Pause.)* Better still, have two drinks. One with me here, and one down the pub later. A group of us are going on there. *(Pause.)* Not that I should drink. My doctor says it's my worst weakness.

PETER: *(Pointing to the papers.)* I've got this work -

MICHAEL: *(Flirting.)* Are you turning me down?

PETER: Of course not.

MICHAEL: *(Moves close to PETER. He looks at him as if he wants to kiss him. The next questions are asked very slowly, and should be played with the maximum amount of eroticism.)* So what do you want? *(Pause.)* Wine? Or do you want juice?

PETER: *(Moves away, a little confused. Quietly.)* Wine.

MICHAEL: I'll go and get it.

PETER: *(As if to break the erotic charge.)* You like running around?

MICHAEL: I haven't done my six o-clock run round the park. This will compensate.

PETER: Do you do that? Run round the park every day?

MICHAEL: Mmm. *(Pause.)* I like it. Don't look so surprised. It's one of the things they urge us to do, isn't it? It's on the menu of right things.

PETER: S'pose so.

MICHAEL: Well! One out of ten for enthusiasm. Who hasn't been reading their menu?

PETER: I think there's some misunderstanding here.

MICHAEL: Yes. I thought you got your good figure from taking care of it.

PETER: Nope. I abuse it, and I guess I don't care too much how it shapes up.

MICHAEL: Looks good to me. *(Puts a finger to his lips.)* But shhh. Careless talk will get you banned. We don't admit to abuse in our group.

PETER: What sort of abuse?

MICHAEL: Oh, the big no-no's. Poppers, alcohol, suppressants. Not to mention the more attractive drugs. *(Sighs.)* Oh, for cocaine again.

PETER: *(Looks shocked.)* Do you mean that?

MICHAEL: Of course I don't mean it. I got a whiff of nitrates on a dance floor and nearly passed out, and got turned on by a cake with hash in it that wasn't meant for me. Hardly abusive living that.

PETER: *(Slowly.)* So...so you take care of yourself?

MICHAEL: I try.

PETER: Michael, there's some misunderstanding.

MICHAEL: What?

PETER: *(Goes silent. Long pause.)* Never mind. How about the wine?

MICHAEL: I'll run.

(While MICHAEL is out of the room PETER goes to a phone and dials.)

PETER: *(Speaking into the phone.)* Hello. Hello is that you Jim? I'm working late here. I've been asked to join the visiting BP group for a drink at the pub, so I'll be late. Don't hold food. *(Pause.)* Yes, I know I'm not supposed to be there. *(Pause.)* Please don't give me a lecture. It's only for a drink - OK? *(Pause.)* Jim, really...*(MICHAEL re-enters and watches him talk on the phone.)*...it's OK. Trust me. *(Puts down phone.)*

MICHAEL: I heard the name Jim. Your lover?

PETER: A friend I was going to have dinner with. *(Pause. Looks guilty.)* I'm sorry I lied to you before. I haven't eaten.

MICHAEL: You cancelled?

PETER: I said not to hold the food.

MICHAEL: Then we can have dinner together. After the pub. *(PETER still looks hesitant.)* Oh come on, I'm over here at your helpline. A visiting relation. You must be kind to us - *(Smiles.)* - to me.

PETER: Are you making a pass at me?

MICHAEL: Thought that was obvious.

PETER: *(Smiles.)* It is obvious. Thanks.

MICHAEL: Thanks!

PETER: For making it clear. *(Pause.)* I'm slow.

MICHAEL: I'll teach you to catch up. *(Offers PETER the wine.)* Drink up.

PETER: *(Takes the glass slowly.)* How many of you came over to visit?

MICHAEL: Well you should know.

PETER: I don't know.

MICHAEL: Twelve. Thirteen counting me.

PETER: Lucky number. Or is it unlucky? I can never remember.

MICHAEL: I am a lucky number. *(Pause.)* I'm well.

PETER: That's good.

(Silence.)

MICHAEL: *(Suddenly serious.)* Why am I lying to you?
          (Pause.) I'm not that well. There have been -
          how shall I say? - certain developments.

PETER: Oh.

MICHAEL: And you?

PETER: Me?

MICHAEL: Yes. Your health.

PETER: No...no developments - as far as I know.

MICHAEL: Seems you've got the lucky number.

PETER: *(Changing the subject.)* What do you do?
          Work, I mean.

MICHAEL: They unemployed me. I was made redundant.
          Clothes company went out of business.

PETER: You like clothes?

MICHAEL: I like style. I followed fashion without ever
          catching up with it. Bought mens fashion
          mags every month until I thought I could
          design and sell as well as them - if not better.

PETER: What happened?

MICHAEL: I took my ideas to a company that had lots of
          ambition. But they lost money, blamed me
          and I lost out.

PETER: Sounds unfair.

MICHAEL: Now I find it hard to work long hours.

PETER: I see.

MICHAEL: *(Brightly.)* I'm not rich, but I can buy you
          dinner. *(Pause.)* Anyway what do you do?

PETER: I work here. I'm a receptionist.

MICHAEL: So that's why you weren't with the Body
            Positive group? They overwork you. I'll
            complain.

PETER: No, please don't.

MICHAEL: I was only joking.

PETER: *(Pause.)* Can I tell you that I'd like to have
            dinner with you? <u>Really</u> like to.

MICHAEL: I thought it was already decided.

PETER: There's been a misunderstanding.

MICHAEL: You do have a lover.

PETER: No, not that.

MICHAEL: The rest I'll forgive you.

PETER: I hope so.

(Long Pause.)

MICHAEL: Hey, this seriousness is killing the romance.
            (Pause.) And I am getting romantic about you.

PETER: *(Quietly.)* Me too.

MICHAEL: I like you.

PETER: Me too.

MICHAEL: Better.

PETER: But I have to tell you - *(Pause.)* - about the
            Body Positive group.

MICHAEL: *(Laughing.)* It's not good?

PETER: Please.

MICHAEL: I'll be serious. Go on.

PETER: I'm not a member of the group. *(Pause. Long
            look at MICHAEL.)* I don't qualify.

SCENE TWO

(MICHAEL's flat. A few hours later. MICHAEL and PETER have just finished a meal. MICHAEL drinks. PETER watches him, almost disapprovingly.)

MICHAEL: I think I've had too much to drink.

PETER: I can see.

MICHAEL: Mmm.

PETER: *(Pause.)* It's getting late. I'm glad you invited me over.

MICHAEL: I realised I couldn't afford to take you out for a meal after all. *(Laughs.)*

PETER: Am I supposed to believe that?

MICHAEL: Told you I was poor. Housing benefit and Invalidity benefit don't go far. *(Pause.)* I've talked too much. I've spent hours telling you what a good clothes designer I could have been.

PETER: *(Stands.)* I'm sure you could be still. And that'll be your seventh glass of wine.

MICHAEL: Been counting?

PETER: It's none of my business but it seems to me you drink a lot.

MICHAEL: You don't approve of drinking?

PETER: Not when it does harm. You said your doctor-

MICHAEL: OK. Sit down. Stay a while longer. Stop me from getting drunk.

(PETER sits. MICHAEL stares at his glass.)

MICHAEL: My mother drinks. She has lots of men friends and she drinks. *(Pause.)* She has her reasons. Anyway, don't for pity's sake get me talking about my mother.

PETER: I'll stay if you don't have that seventh glass of wine.

MICHAEL: Emotional blackmail already?

PETER: *(Quietly.)* Yes.

MICHAEL: I like that.

PETER: Is it a deal?

MICHAEL: *(Pushes away bottle.)* It's a deal. Just because it's you, and because - oh well...so tell me about you.

PETER: But I want to hear about you.

MICHAEL: That will bring me back to my family. I was born in the sixties when my mother was swinging a bit higher than she is swinging now, and my father was - *(Pause.)* - let's leave out my father.

PETER: You make him sound more of a mystery than your mother.

MICHAEL: Not a mystery at all. He's an unhappy man. I love him very much. I could spend whole evenings talking about him.

PETER: *(Smiles.)* I'm invited back?

MICHAEL: Depends if you tell me about you. Childhood is always good as a starter. Beginnings and all that.

PETER: My beginnings were dull. I was a dull child. I lived in South London, had the sort of education that got me through Grammar

School to A-levels. Then I went into various jobs in the City. *(Pause.)* Dull.

MICHAEL: You've overworked the word.

PETER: It's true.

MICHAEL: When did you discover you were gay?

PETER: There was this boy who fainted in the school playground. I was thirteen. He was twelve. Instead of undoing his collar to give him breathing space, I undid his trousers.

MICHAEL: *(Laughing.)* Where did you manage to do that?

PETER: A group of us carried him off to the playground toilet. The rest got bored and left me alone with him. *(Pause.)* I wasn't bored. He came round to me giving him a rather intense examination of his lower regions.

MICHAEL: *(Still laughing.)* However did you become dull after that?

PETER: He slapped my face. Called me a pervert. I Spent the rest of my teenage years doing penance with a lot of boring girls.

MICHAEL: And then?

PETER: *(Stands.)* Now I need a drink.

(MICHAEL stands. Long pause. PETER goes to him and caresses his face.)

PETER: May I?

MICHAEL: It's a nice feeling.

PETER: May I - *(Pause.)* - kiss you?

MICHAEL: As long as I can kiss you back.

(They kiss. PETER draws away.)

MICHAEL: Disappointed?

PETER: Can we kiss please?

MICHAEL: I thought we had.

PETER: Properly.

MICHAEL: I kiss badly.

PETER: I am sure you don't always kiss with your lips
           closed.

MICHAEL: *(Awkward.)* Look I -

PETER: I want to kiss you.

(Pause.)

MICHAEL: Peter, you are not -

PETER: No, I'm not HIV. Or rather I don't know if I'm
           HIV. I behave as if I am. I also believe there is
           no risk in kissing with our mouths open.
           (Pause.) Oh this is absurd. Everything I'll
           have to say on the subject will sound wrong.

MICHAEL: No, please - don't let's make a big thing out of
           it. Not now. If we do we'll ruin it. Of course I
           know there's no risk in open-mouth kissing. I
           don't even know why I behave like that. Old
           fears. Reflex. Fears die slowly.

PETER: So let's -

(Long pause.)

MICHAEL: Yes. Let's -

PETER: Let's go to bed. Please? *(Smiles.)* I'm more
           advanced than I was in the school playground.

MICHAEL: *(Laughs.)* Sure? Not dull?

PETER: I promise I won't be dull if you encourage me.
           (Pause.) Let's be - natural with each other.

MICHAEL: *(Goes to PETER and caresses him.)* May I
          just have one more glass of wine first?

BLACKOUT

SCENE THREE

*(ADAM's flat. A few days later. MICHAEL and ADAM on
stage. It's clear they have just had sex. ADAM is naked.
MICHAEL is dressing.)*

ADAM: I think he should have told you.

MICHAEL: He did tell me.

ADAM: Then why did you go on seeing him?

MICHAEL: Isn't that a pretty narrow-minded question?

ADAM: I didn't like the way he got involved with us
          that's all. *(Pause.)* He wasn't invited.

MICHAEL: I invited him.

ADAM: You?

MICHAEL: I invited him to join us. Does it matter?

ADAM: Then he latched on to you. *(Pause.)* He found
          you attractive.

MICHAEL: *(Laughs.)* Is that a crime?

ADAM: I don't see it like you do. *(Pause.)* I see it as -

MICHAEL: As what?

ADAM: Exploitation.

MICHAEL: That's ridiculous. *(Getting angry.)* Look shall
          we take this point by point?

ADAM: I don't think that's necessary. You know what
          I mean.

MICHAEL: That's what worries me. It also worries me
that part of me has been trained to believe
you. *(Pause.)* I'm HIV and I have to be careful
I'm not exploited sexually or emotionally by a
guy who says he isn't. Or in Peter's case, a guy
who hasn't tested and doesn't know. *(Pause.)*
Where is the exploitation? *(Smiles.)* My
vulnerability?

ADAM: It's not funny.

MICHAEL: It's sodding sad. *(Pause.)* It also works the
other way round. How many men have you
exploited? Or me for that matter! Gone to bed
with, had sex with, even risky sex with, and
not told them you were HIV?

ADAM: Maybe I did - before.

MICHAEL: Before what? Our new book of morals?

ADAM: We don't have a book of morals.

MICHAEL: We seem to have a lot of inner police.

ADAM: Michael, he knew you were HIV. He knew the
whole group of us were. When he joined us
we thought he was too. We said things -
confidential things. We assumed he was one
of us.

MICHAEL: I am not one of anything. I am me.

ADAM: We assumed he was HIV. If we had known he
wasn't we would have talked about...

MICHAEL: The weather?

ADAM: It's serious, Michael.

MICHAEL: He is hardly going to spread it around that the
people we introduced him to are HIV. Now is
he? For a start he'd never remember the
names. *(ADAM shrugs his shoulders.)* Well?

ADAM: Maybe not.

MICHAEL: Of course not.

ADAM: But if we don't keep to the rules -

MICHAEL: Back to the unwritten book of our new
             morality. *(Pause.)* Thou shalt not fraternise
             unknowingly with a fellow gay unless he has
             revealed his antibody status.

(Long pause.)

ADAM: And what about you?

MICHAEL: What about me?

ADAM: Are you serious about him?

MICHAEL: I'm thinking about him. *(Pause.)* Yes, I feel I
             could be serious about him.

ADAM: Personally, I feel it's easier to have sexual
             relationships with people who know from the
             inside how we are feeling.

MICHAEL: God is not available.

ADAM: Smart.

MICHAEL: Or our counsellors.

ADAM: We do have each other.

MICHAEL: Others who are also HIV? I still like to think I
             have a broader field, thank you. *(Pause.)* And
             sharing someone else's fear of falling ill is not
             fun.

ADAM: Neither is sharing someone else's fear of <u>you</u>
             falling ill.

MICHAEL: *(Quietly.)* You are a good friend Adam, and
             I'd even call you my best friend, but I think I
             want to call a halt to this conversation.

(Long uncomfortable pause.)

ADAM: We had something special. You and I.

MICHAEL: Yes, we had something special. *(Pause.)* Is this the reason for this moral lecture?

ADAM: *(Smiles.)* Would I be that obvious?

MICHAEL: Yes.

ADAM: Partly.

MICHAEL: *(Quietly.)* What do you feel?

ADAM: *(Slightly mocking.)* I want to carry you away to that safe place where we will live happily ever after. On a horse of course.

MICHAEL: Charming. Prince Charming. But you won't move me to want us to get back together. Sorry.

ADAM: It was worth a try.

MICHAEL: Better friendship.

ADAM: Ah, friendship. That reserved place for the rejected you still want to have around you. *(Pause.)* Fortunately I still want you around me.

MICHAEL: Then stop worrying about my welfare.

ADAM: He may hurt you.

MICHAEL: My risk.

ADAM: Not a risk I like. I still love you. *(Pause.)* If he hurts you, we as a group pick up the pieces.

MICHAEL: He may not hurt me. I may hurt him. *(Pause.)* He is a person you know, even if his blood count is perhaps slightly different from ours.

BLACKOUT

SCENE FOUR

(MICHAEL's flat. Weeks later. MICHAEL is alone on stage reading a book. The Doorbell rings. MICHAEL goes to door. PETER enters with a bunch of yellow flowers.)

PETER: I hope you like...

MICHAEL: *(Smiles.)* Flowers. It's been such a long time since I got flowers I've forgotten how to put them in a vase. *(Slight pause.)* Thank you.

PETER: Giving presents is hell. Have you ever thought of that?

MICHAEL: *(Takes flowers.)* Yes.

PETER: I mean - what do you give? A box of chocolates? Men aren't taught to give other men presents. Chocolates, flowers, that sort of thing. They've taught us that's men to women stuff. *(Pause.)* As for women they usually end up giving the wrong tie, or the wrong shirt, or the wrong eau de cologne. It's hopeless. *(Pause.)* Supposing I'd brought you the wrong eau de cologne?

MICHAEL: *(Laughing.)* I'd have kicked you out!

PETER: So I end up with flowers. You've got yellow blinds in your bedroom so I thought the flowers would match and we could look at them in bed.

MICHAEL: *(Puts the flowers to one side.)* I'm glad there's an ulterior motive.

PETER: The best.

(Long pause.)

PETER: Did I say something wrong?

MICHAEL: No, of course not.

PETER: Sure?

MICHAEL: Sure.

(Long silence.)

PETER: If we keep up this silence the flowers will
          have wilted, then I won't see them from the
          bed.

MICHAEL: *(Slowly.)* I saw my doctor today. At the
          hospital.

PETER: I knew you were going. I'd hoped you'd let me
          come along with you.

MICHAEL: I thought about it, but I had a visit to make on
          the ward.

PETER: *(Goes to him.)* Are you OK?

MICHAEL: *(Moves away.)* I'm OK. What happened on the
          ward upset me. It's nothing unusual.

PETER: I'm sorry.

MICHAEL: What I'm trying to say is I don't want you in at
          the deep end.

PETER: I can swim.

MICHAEL: Seriously.

PETER: What <u>are</u> you trying to say?

MICHAEL: The hospital. Going along with me. *(Pause.)*
          What's happening to me.

PETER: Can you tell me what's happening? I want to
          know.

MICHAEL: My blood count is low. *(Pause.)* I've lost
          weight. Not a lot, but a little is always a lot
          when you're HIV.

PETER: Yes.

(Long pause.)

MICHAEL: It could be to do with stress.

PETER: You mean me?

MICHAEL: Don't get me wrong. I want you. I know you want me. My doctor assured me that what we do is alright, that - *(Pause.)*

PETER: Well, then?

MICHAEL: It's what you suggested the other day about moving in. That's stress.

PETER: *(Making a joke of it.)* I have a low paid job, you don't get much income. We need all the money we can get. Paying one rent is better than two. Think of it - we'll both have more spending money!

MICHAEL: Is that the best argument for it? *(Smiles.)* You're fun, do you know that? And I'm fast becoming a miserable bastard. All resemblance to that guy you met at the BP party is purely coincidental.

PETER: I'll cheer you up. *(Pause.)* Morning and night, and anytime in between.

MICHAEL: But Peter, think of the future.

PETER: I am. There's a telephone bill coming in the post any day. I want to avoid paying it.

MICHAEL: Will you be serious?

PETER: Time enough for that once I've unpacked my bags.

MICHAEL: *(Slowly.)* Do you have much stuff?

PETER: Ah - constructive interest.

MICHAEL: Do you?

PETER: You've seen my room. I'll leave her the lamp.
            The rest is mine. About three suitcases worth.
            (Pause.) A couple of hours packing, half an
            hour in a taxi, and I'm all yours!

MICHAEL: I'm a bad sleeper.

PETER: *(Laughing.)* Don't care.

MICHAEL: I snore.

PETER: So do I.

MICHAEL: I make dreadful toast.

PETER: I'll survive.

MICHAEL: *(Looks at him steadily.)* I also have bad night
            sweats.

PETER: I'll wipe you down.

MICHAEL: I often scream in the night.

PETER: I'll hold you close.

(Long pause.)

MICHAEL: You really mean all this, don't you?

PETER: Look, you came into the office where I work,
            you sweep me off my feet - in fact you
            seduced me, and now, now you have the
            cheek to try and put me off! *(Pause.)* Young
            man, I won't be trifled with!

MICHAEL: *(Almost a sob in his voice.)* This is madness.

PETER: Best things are.

MICHAEL: No, no they're not. The stress factor -

PETER: You won't have one once you accept the fact
            you can't live without me.

MICHAEL: Peter -

PETER: OK, so you can live without me, but you can do with the rent. I can understand love not winning, but money?

MICHAEL: You've used that argument.

PETER: It's a good repeat.

MICHAEL: *(Goes to him, caresses his cheek.)* How long will it take you to move in?

PETER: You serious?

MICHAEL: I'm serious.

PETER: *(Pause.)* About a minute.

MICHAEL: *(Laughs.)* What?

PETER: I said about a minute.

MICHAEL: I thought you had three suitcases -

PETER: I have. I knew I had all the best arguments on my side, so -

MICHAEL: I think I'm beginning to see the point of all this.

PETER: You've guessed right. It was bloody murder carrying them up the stairs with the flowers. They're outside the door.

BLACKOUT

SCENE FIVE

(MICHAEL's flat. A few days later. MICHAEL, alone on stage, sitting on a chair facing the audience.)

MICHAEL: I can talk now you're asleep. *(Pause.)* I wish I could sleep, Peter, but after what I saw yesterday there is no way I can close my eyes. That last sleep of his was so sudden. *(Pause.)* A young kid. I liked him. I desired him. He came on to that ward chirpy and full of jokes like he was taking time out for a rest from a party. Nineteen years old. The only sign he had pneumonia that first day he arrived was that he was a little breathless, like an ordinary young guy would get running up a flight of stairs two at a time. *(Long pause.)* His lover was with him every day. Distressed but knowing he'd come out. They laughed and they joked, and even when the nurses put the oxygen mask on his face to help him breathe he was still smiling with his eyes. Then one day his parents visited, and they invited me to eat with them. Billy was well enough to sit on the balcony of his room. The sun was bright and warm and it was like a picnic. His lover held his hand and even tried to feed him strawberries. I thought, this is the ideal picture. Lovers happy, parents caring. I thought the sun won't ever go in. *(Longer pause.)* Yesterday I arrived at the hospital at noon. Peter, I did consider taking you with me because I thought it would be a happy day. I wanted you to see them together, happy with each other. *(Pause.)* A nurse stopped me in front of his door. Billy had died, suddenly, half an hour before. He had had a bronchoscopy, that stupid, painful investigation of the lungs, and he had died. The nurse was sorry they had thrust that thing down his throat, but there was no bringing him back. She told me they had taken him away already, which I didn't believe, and after she had gone I disobeyed her and went into his room. *(Pause.)* Billy was a short, cute guy, his body so compact it was made for dancing. He was there on the bed but sealed up in a bag

like a parcel waiting to be picked up. The bag
seemed so small I could hardly believe he was
inside it. The sun beat down on the bag, and I
thought stupidly how hot he must be inside.
(Long pause. Cries out.) What do I have to do,
Peter, to drive you away so that you never see
me like that?

BLACKOUT

SCENE SIX

*(MICHAEL's flat. A few days later. MICHAEL is seated on
the floor with a box of books beside him. There is a small
pile of books which he is slowly placing into the box.
PETER is watching him.)*

PETER: You don't have to do that.

MICHAEL: They are taking up cupboard space you need.
It's not important.

PETER: It makes me feel I'm taking over the flat.

MICHAEL: It's not important. *(Turns to PETER.)* Have
you unpacked everything?

PETER: Only the stuff I need.

MICHAEL: Well, that's the point isn't it? You haven't got
enough space to put your things.

PETER: I don't want to put you out.

MICHAEL: Either we are living together or we are not. If
we are then it's equal space.

PETER: It's your flat.

MICHAEL: This is silly. Just because you need space for
your things doesn't mean you are taking over.

PETER: I know, but -

MICHAEL: So far we haven't had an argument. Don't let's start our living together arguing over something as trivial as this.

PETER: They're your things. They are not trivial. What are you going to do with the box?

MICHAEL: It can go under the bed.

PETER: <u>My</u> things could go under the bed.

MICHAEL: Clothes are for cupboards, Peter. These books are taking up cupboard space. You can't put clothes under a bed. *(Pause.)* Now can we stop talking about this?

PETER: It seems unfair.

MICHAEL: *(Stands up.)* Why don't you make us both a cup of tea?

PETER: I'm not happy about what you are doing.

MICHAEL: It's a small flat. You need space. I am making space.

PETER: Seeing you do that makes me feel like an intruder.

MICHAEL: *(Emphatically.)* Tea, Peter.

PETER: *(Moves towards him.)* I'd rather make love.

MICHAEL: *(Backs away.)* You always want to make love.

PETER: I don't call once a day excessive.

MICHAEL: *(Smiles.)* Honeymoon time, eh?

PETER: No. It's not something I imagine us getting bored with.

MICHAEL: Sometimes I get tired -

PETER: Then you must tell me, lie back and let me do all the work. *(Pause.)* Sorry. I didn't express that properly.

MICHAEL: Why do you need sex every day, Peter?

PETER: *(Looks shocked.)* What?

MICHAEL: Why do you need sex every day?

PETER: I happen to be in love with you. I only have to come near you and I want to touch you. Caress you. I've never felt this before with anyone.

MICHAEL: Sometimes we use sex to verify our feelings.

PETER: Christ, Michael. You don't think I'm doing that, do you?

MICHAEL: I know you want to make love to me, but I get the impression you are proving something to yourself.

(Silence. PETER paces the room.)

PETER: *(Looks angrily at MICHAEL.)* That's not true.

MICHAEL: I shouldn't have said that.

PETER: It's just we haven't made love in three days.

MICHAEL: The moving in, the stress. I haven't felt like it.

PETER: Before I moved in we went to bed every day. It was fun. It was good for both of us. There was no verifying feelings -

MICHAEL: I'm sorry I said that.

PETER: If I was over demanding then why didn't you say so?

MICHAEL: Your enthusiasm was - how shall I put it - overwhelming.

PETER: So you don't want us to do it every day?

MICHAEL: That's too black and white. You should be able to sense when I <u>want</u> it. You should also be able to sense when I <u>don't</u> want it.

PETER: Like now.

MICHAEL: Stress turns me off.

PETER: What about when you sense that I want it?

MICHAEL: We have to learn to make love when we both want to. That goes both ways. When we both want sex then it'll be alright. It's no good us doing it for the other person.

PETER: *(Slowly.)* Do you enjoy making love to me?

MICHAEL: I'm not answering that Peter.

PETER: Why?

MICHAEL: It's obvious I'd have thought.

PETER: That you do?

MICHAEL: No, I hate every minute of it.

PETER: I'm being serious.

MICHAEL: You are being insecure.

PETER: Yes.

MICHAEL: Don't be.

PETER: *(Picks up a book and opens it.)* This is all very new, isn't it?

MICHAEL: I haven't lived with anyone before, if that's what you mean.

PETER: Neither have I.

MICHAEL: *(Trying to change the subject.)* Now I'd better finish off doing this job.

PETER: Did you ever want to live with anyone else?

MICHAEL: Peter, I'm tired. I don't really want to talk about important things. Let's just get on with what we have to do.

PETER: I'm talking too much?

MICHAEL: I didn't say that either.

PETER: *(Closes book and puts it back into the pile.)* I love you.

MICHAEL: *(Quietly.)* I know.

PETER: I'll go and make some tea.

(PETER moves to go. MICHAEL catches his arm.)

MICHAEL: Not yet.

PETER: I thought you wanted some tea.

MICHAEL: Kiss me.

PETER: *(Laughs.)* Now you are confusing me.

MICHAEL: Kiss me.

(They kiss. MICHAEL breaks away and returns to sorting out the books. Silence.)

PETER: It's good between us, isn't it?

MICHAEL: You know that.

PETER: I mean, I can't believe in a way that I'm here, actually here, living with you. I could dance I feel so happy.

MICHAEL: It's late and we do have neighbours.

PETER: The feeling makes me want to dance. *(Pause.)* Now I'm being too enthusiastic again.

MICHAEL: The Chinese say beware of enthusiasm.

PETER: I don't know any Chinese.

MICHAEL: Confucius said it.

PETER: Did he? Well, he was an ancient man of wisdom, so he should have known! *(He points to books.)* You're not burying him in the box, are you?

MICHAEL: Enthusiasm often doesn't last.

PETER: Michael, I thought you didn't want to talk about important things? *(MICHAEL is silent.)* Are you saying in a polite way that my enthusiastic feelings might not last?

MICHAEL: Make some tea.

PETER: Please answer me.

MICHAEL: I meant generally.

PETER: Yes, but specifically I am enthusiastic.

MICHAEL: Don't read more into it -

PETER: *(Interrupting.)* I mean I want to feel like this for always.

MICHAEL: I don't think in terms of always, Peter. You shouldn't either.

PETER: You mean the "nothing lasts forever" bit?

MICHAEL: Well, there is proof since the beginning of time that things don't.

PETER: Okay, so it's an illusion, but I like the word "always". I <u>know</u> things change. *(Pause.)* We grow old, we die - *(Stops.)*

(Silence.)

MICHAEL: Go on.

PETER: I can't imagine my feelings changing for you.

MICHAEL: *(Icily.)* We <u>die</u>, Peter.

PETER: *(Quietly, half turning away.)* Yes, I know.

MICHAEL: One day I am going to die, probably before you, and then your feelings will have to change. None of this can go on forever. *(Points to the box.)* We put things away when things change.

PETER: Not feelings.

MICHAEL: Feelings too.

PETER: It's not true for everyone.

MICHAEL: I have never known an exception.

PETER: Maybe I am it.

MICHAEL: Maybe.

PETER: Yes. *(Holds MICHAEL close.)* Yes, I am the exception.

MICHAEL: *(Pushes him away gently.)* I am getting very tired. Better give up on the books tonight. We have plenty of time -

PETER: That's right.

MICHAEL: - to do the job. *(Looks at PETER.)* Oh don't look so down. I hate it when you look down. *(Pause. Smiles.)* I prefer you dancing.

PETER: Do you?

MICHAEL: Mind you, I've never seen you dance.

PETER: I'm not sure if I'm any good.

MICHAEL: *(Slowly.)* I was, before the tiredness.

PETER: We'll go to a club together.

MICHAEL: I'd like that.

PETER: *(Looks at MICHAEL.)* I don't want anyone to touch my body except you, Michael. Ever.

BLACKOUT

SCENE SIX

(MICHAEL'S FATHER's house. FATHER seated. MICHAEL standing.)

MICHAEL: I hoped you'd want to see me.

FATHER: I never said I didn't want to see you. Quite the opposite.

MICHAEL: Where's mother?

FATHER: Out with my replacement. Do I have to draw you a picture? *(Pause.)* The last time you came she was out. The man was different.

MICHAEL: I'm sorry.

FATHER: I'm not. For the past five years she's only been good at making my tea. *(Pause.)* Talk to me.

MICHAEL: I've met someone. I'm living with him.

FATHER: I don't think I'm qualified to talk about that.

MICHAEL: I want to talk to you about it. I feel close to you.

FATHER: I still don't think I'm qualified. *(Smiles.)* Anyway, I think anybody living together is a mistake.

MICHAEL: When Mum refused to listen, you listened. I could always talk to you about the men I'd met.

FATHER: We haven't talked about the men you've met since the diagnosis. *(Pause.)* You're a risk now aren't you?

MICHAEL: What?

FATHER: A risk. An Aids risk. To whoever he is. *(Pause.)* What is his name?

MICHAEL: Peter. *(Pause.)* He wants to take it on board, and anyway there are things we can do that are not -

FATHER: You mean the safer sex stuff?

MICHAEL: It's true certain things are safe.

FATHER: *(Angrily)* What do they know? What do you know?

MICHAEL: Do you expect me to just stop then?

FATHER: I don't know. *(Pause.)* Maybe you had better make the tea. It's a hot day.

MICHAEL: I want to talk to you about this.

FATHER: I told you - I'm not qualified. I brought you and one of your boyfriends breakfast in bed. That's as far as I go.

MICHAEL: *(Quietly.)* You've known this yourself haven't you?

(Silence.)

FATHER: If you're inferring -

MICHAEL: His name was Al. He came for a meal when I was a child. He looked at me - well, like he wanted me to be his son.

FATHER: Nonsense.

MICHAEL: Is it?

FATHER: Yes. *(Pause.)* Al was the best man at the wedding. He has always been -

MICHAEL: The best man?

(Long silence.)

FATHER: Alright. We played around. A long time ago. In the sixties. He wanted it to be long term. I liked women more, I suppose. Then it stopped, and I married your mother. *(Pause.)* There wasn't Aids around then.

MICHAEL: It doesn't alter feelings.

FATHER: Doesn't it? Then why are you here? Questioning me about how you should feel?

MICHAEL: Because I thought you could imagine how I was feeling.

FATHER: I've got no imagination.

MICHAEL: Could you stop?

FATHER: What?

MICHAEL: Sex.

FATHER: That's a joke. I have. When was the last time I had it? I certainly don't touch your mother - and I don't go after other women.

MICHAEL: What if Al appeared?

FATHER: Al was teenage nonsense. You went with girls when you were eighteen. You grew out of them. I grew out of him.

MICHAEL: Did you?

FATHER: Yes. I did. Seriously I did. *(Pause.)* And I can't help you. I don't understand it enough. *(Looks hard at MICHAEL.)* Does Peter still want you, knowing you're infected?

MICHAEL: That I've got HIV.

FATHER: Sorry. That you've got HIV.

MICHAEL: Yes.

FATHER: Then he feels something?

MICHAEL: *(Smiles.)* I'm not sure. Sometimes I feel I'm the human extension of a cause. He wants to do good.

FATHER: That's harsh.

MICHAEL: It's trendy now to want to do good.

FATHER: I wouldn't have thought dying was trendy.

MICHAEL: He doesn't imagine dying.

FATHER: Well he won't imagine it if what you say is true - if there's no risk.

(Long pause.)

MICHAEL: I keep on telling myself there's no risk, for him, for me. Then I wonder how far I am down the spectrum. How far I have to go. Already I've got Thrush. Some people say the barrier is crossed once you've got Thrush.

FATHER: You mean? -

MICHAEL: Yes.

FATHER: I don't know what to say. *(Angry.)* I don't want you to be sick. I don't want you to look sick. *(Long pause.)* Make the tea. Let me absorb all this. *(Pause.)* Is he a nice person this Peter?

MICHAEL: Can you ever tell?

FATHER: There are signs.

MICHAEL: He wants to be.

FATHER: Will you let him? *(Reaches out and holds MICHAEL's hand.)*

MICHAEL: That's unfair. *(Takes away his hand.)*

FATHER: I hope you give him a chance. *(Reaches out again.)*

BLACKOUT

SCENE SEVEN

(TIM's house. PETER and TIM. TIM is putting away some surgical instruments. PETER is watching him while pacing the room.)

PETER: How did you cope?

TIM: When Anne died of cancer? *(Pause.)* I'm a doctor remember. Doctors are supposed to cope. Except that I made hell out of all my relationships outside of the surgery. *(Pause.)* God was I hell with people.

PETER: You weren't hell with me. You didn't even tell me.

TIM: I didn't trust men with emotions then. *(Pause.)* Now I'm admitting perhaps I was wrong. But we aren't talking about Anne and I, we are talking about you and Michael.

PETER: What did you think about him when you met him?

TIM: I found him as closed in, as buttoned up as you are. You are both good room pacers. *(Pause.)* Do you talk about it?

PETER: Aids?

TIM: More your relationship. Or are you saying Aids is your relationship?

PETER: Sometimes it feels like it's all there is.

TIM: Well it clearly isn't. It's obvious you love him.

PETER: Tell him that!

TIM: *(Sits down.)* Peter will you sit down? *(PETER sits.)* It's not easy telling a person whose wounds are clearly visible that the wounds are lovable. He is one big hurt as far as I can

	make out, and you are fast getting like him. *(Pause.)* Do you ever have a laugh together?

PETER: We used to have lots of laughs together.

TIM: Then arrange to go out one night a week just for laughs.

PETER: Not easy.

TIM: Make it easy. Make it flippant. Make something fun. *(Pause.)* Go one weekend to the seaside. Go play on the funfair. Go on the ghost train.

PETER: He's told me what to expect. How it could be.

TIM: You mean the possible deterioration?

PETER: The very real deterioration.

TIM: And?

PETER: I just stood there saying clichés. I felt like screaming inside. Except I didn't. I just said the first stupid things that came into my mouth, and he knew I wasn't telling the truth.

TIM: *(Smiles.)* What is telling the truth?

PETER: Not lies.

TIM: I'm sure you didn't lie to him.

PETER: I lied to him. *(Pause.)* I wanted to say that I was scared of losing him. That I wouldn't have gone into a relationship with him if I had seriously considered at the beginning the fear of losing him.

TIM: Is that true?

PETER: It's all muddled. Yes. No. *(Pause.)* As he reminded me he's got good muscles, strong limbs. I couldn't imagine them getting flabby, becoming thin.

TIM: And now you can?

PETER: Yes.

TIM: I couldn't imagine making love to Anne with
           one breast when they had to cut one off, but
           we made love. She wanted it. I wanted it.

(Long silence.)

TIM: I saw that about Michael.

PETER: What?

TIM: He looks like a man who enjoys making love.
           (Pause.) But he will have to trust you. Trust
           that you want him, even when he isn't like he
           is now.

PETER: Supposing I let myself down?

TIM: Making love to someone who may die can
           mean so many things. Essentially, it's the
           assurance of wanting more than anything else.
           (Pause.) Demands change.

PETER: I know and admit it's irrational, but what if I
           get the virus?

TIM: You take precautions, don't you?

PETER: Yes.

TIM: Well?

PETER: The old habit of fear. *(Long pause.)* The first
           time I kissed him with our mouths open I felt I
           was going to pass out. Total irrational fear.
           Not that I showed it. He gave me a dry kiss
           first. It was me who forced him to kiss me
           with his mouth open. There was his saliva
           meeting mine, and there too in my brain was
           this stupid scenario - healthy wet meets
           unhealthy wet. I kissed the virus when we first

kissed. *(Pause.)* Two people who know the facts, and yet are still controlled by out-dated fears.

TIM: And now?

PETER: It's still there, for me, as it probably is for him, but I want to kiss him so much. I couldn't not kiss him. *(Pause.)* The brain is beginning to learn to shut up, to let me get on with enjoying him. *(Pause.)* That's the difference, Tim. You and Anne. There was the loss, the disfigurement, but you didn't feel you'd possibly lose your life as well.

TIM: That's true, but I thought more of her life than of my own.

PETER: Did you?

TIM: Yes. Yes, I did - most of the time. *(Pause.)* Do you know what you need?

PETER: What?

TIM: A place to scream in. The best book I've read on Aids. This mother about to lose her son. *(Pause.)* She kept sane by having a place to scream in. I don't know, or can't recall if it was real or imaginary, but she had this place to go and let all the pain out. You need that.

PETER: I can't scream. *(Pause.)*

TIM: Tried?

PETER: No.

TIM: Try.

PETER: Now?

TIM: I'm here.

PETER: *(Embarrassed.)* I'll get my own place. Do it alone.

TIM: See if you can do it first. *(Pause.)* Trust me. Trust me enough to let out a scream. You want to. Let the burning out.

PETER: He's made me so cold.

(Long pause.)

TIM: What's the worst fear?

PETER: About Aids?

TIM: About how it affects you both.

PETER: Losing him.

TIM: Visualise it.

PETER: Can't.

TIM: Try.

PETER: The image is too painful.

TIM: So you do have an image?

PETER: Yes. *(Pause.)* It's a room.

TIM: Feel it. Feel the image. Don't think about it any more. Feel it.

PETER: What was the worst image you had about Anne?

TIM: I'm talking about you.

PETER: I want you to tell me.

TIM: *(After a long pause.)* Seeing that cut off breast lying around in a hospital, and knowing that I had touched it, caressed it, made love to it. Seeing that breast and knowing that it was no longer a part of her and that it would be destroyed.

(PETER starts to scream. A throttled sound at first, then the pain inside shows more strongly. He places his hands on the back of a chair for support and begins to yell. It lasts for a few seconds, then stops. He remains motionless. Long silence.)

PETER: I -

TIM: Don't talk. Not yet.

PETER: *(Nearly crying as he speaks.)* I - I want to say -what I see.

TIM: *(Quietly.)* If you're ready, then begin to tell me.

(Long pause.)

PETER: It's like coming into a beautiful room that you know you would be happy spending the rest of your life in. *(Pause.)* There are a few things to change in the room, but no essentials. *(Pause.)* And then you are told - I am told, that I can't always have the room, that it's only on a short-term lease. That I can love it for as long as the lease lasts. *(Pause.)* You try to bargain - I try to bargain. Try to make deals. Nothing works. The room is mine, temporarily. *(Pause.)* The sun coming through the window of the room is mine temporarily. *(Grips the chair again, opens his mouth to scream, but stops.)*

TIM: Do it again, if it helps.

PETER: *(Shakes his head.)* The things in the room begin to go. Ornaments first, a book here, a record there. Not important. Details. Then it becomes serious. The furniture goes. The chairs, the table, the fire for when there's no warmth from the sun. Then finally the bed itself. The resting place itself is taken away from me. *(Long pause.)* The room is bare, but I still love it. It's still mine. But slowly I have to reconcile myself to leaving the room. It can no longer be sustained by love alone. I can no longer be sustained. It's a cold, empty place. No warmth left. No way to put the warmth back. I have to reconcile myself to closing the door, knowing that nowhere else will ever be as wanted, ever be as needed again. Or loved. *(Long pause.)* From then onwards I know all shelters are to be temporary.

BLACKOUT

SCENE EIGHT

(A field. MICHAEL and PETER. Music. Both make love to the music, then sink down exhausted, but happy.
MICHAEL has his head on PETER's lap. At a distance a picnic basket open with food, plates and cups surrounding it. Behind MICHAEL and PETER a very round, very bright sun.)

(MICHAEL wipes the sweat off his face.)

PETER: Hot?

MICHAEL: Mmm.

PETER: Sound content.

MICHAEL: Mmm.

PETER: Good. *(Bends down and kisses him on the mouth. A passionate kiss.)*

MICHAEL: *(Sits up.)* You know this is the first time I've been out in the countryside since - well, since-

PETER: Since you moved to London?

MICHAEL: Mmm, perhaps. *(Pause.)* No, if I remember right I went to visit a windmill somewhere. The Body Positive group. An outing.

PETER: *(Coldly.)* That sounds fun.

MICHAEL: *(Suspicious.)* Do you mean that?

PETER: *(Defensively.)* Why shouldn't I mean it?

MICHAEL: Don't know. Sounded as if you were knocking it.

(Silence. PETER stands up. Begins to pack away the picnic things.)

MICHAEL: Now you're offended.

PETER: Just when we are happy there's always something we say to spoil it.

MICHAEL: Sorry.

PETER: I wasn't knocking the outing. In fact if you want me to analyze it, and we do analyze practically everything, I was feeling envious.

MICHAEL: Why?

PETER: No, jealous. Jealous that when another outing comes along you can go on it and I can't.

MICHAEL: Lovers can sometimes come with us.

PETER: Yes, but they are not over welcome.

MICHAEL: We need time and space to ourselves, Peter. How many times do I have to tell you that?

PETER: It just seems so separatist.

MICHAEL: We have issues only we can, and want to talk about. *(Pause.)* I want to talk about something else.

PETER: But can't you understand that I might feel
             jealous about not being there with you?
             Sharing the things you share with them?

MICHAEL: So what do you want me to do about it? Infect
             you so you can come along?

PETER: Sometimes I feel I wouldn't mind.

*(MICHAEL stands up. Looks at PETER with cold anger,
then hits him across the face twice.)*

MICHAEL: Don't ever say that again. Do you hear?

PETER: *(Slightly afraid.)* Alright.

MICHAEL: It's not alright. I don't know if you meant it or
             not, and I don't want to know, but don't ever
             say it again. *(Pause.)* It shows - it shows just
             how little you really understand.

PETER: Thank you for the vote of confidence. Maybe
             it shows I envy you for going through
             something I can't go through. There is envy in
             all this, and I'm honest enough to admit it.

MICHAEL: It's not honesty. It's bloody stupid
             romanticism. *(Long pause.)* People who feel
             they are missing out on our great adventure
             are sick in my book.

PETER: It comes down to sharing again.

MICHAEL: You can't share this.

PETER: I love you.

MICHAEL: Then keep your distance, and don't feel
             jealousy and envy because you are excluded
             from the club, 'cos it's not a club I would have
             wanted to join if I had had the choice.

PETER: *(Sits down.)* Lie down with me.

MICHAEL: I'm too angry.

PETER: Lie down with me.

MICHAEL: I don't take orders.

PETER: I'm asking.

MICHAEL: I don't want physical contact with you at the moment.

PETER: Who said I'd touch you?

MICHAEL: OK. *(Sits down.)* Now what?

PETER: You don't particularly like me telling you I love you, do you?

MICHAEL: I'll pass on that.

PETER: Is it the word?

MICHAEL: It's a lot of things.

PETER: Have you ever said it?

MICHAEL: Yes. *(Pause.)* To the guy who gave me the virus.

PETER: *(Quickly.)* So you knew who it was?

MICHAEL: No, I got fucked senseless by twenty-five people a night every night for a year. *(Pause.)* That's the myth, isn't it?

PETER: I didn't mean -

MICHAEL: No. No one ever does. *(Pause.)* I was in love with the guy. I'd had the test regularly. I was in the clear. He told me he was negative, and we fucked without a condom. *(Pause.)* Months later, I showed up positive. I hadn't been with anyone else but him.

PETER: What did you say to him?

MICHAEL: I didn't say anything. He was in Sweden at the time on business, and when he got back I'd moved. I hated him. How I hated him.

>   *(Pause.)* Then some counsellor came out with
>   a bit of unexpected wisdom.

PETER: Like what?

MICHAEL: The difference between chemistry and love.

PETER: *(Smiles.)* I don't follow.

MICHAEL: She said I was in chemistry with him and not
            in love. *(Pause.)* Chemistry is when two
            chemical compatibles get on well in bed, have
            sensible conversations and delude themselves
            it's loving.

PETER: Is this "in chemistry"?

MICHAEL: I don't know.

PETER: To be honest we are not that - well,
            compatible, and who says we ever have
            sensible conversations?

MICHAEL: She had a point.

PETER: I love you. And to be in love means warmth to
            me. *(Points upwards.)* Like the sun. I never
            was much good at chemistry, so I don't know
            if that can answer wanting to be warm with
            someone. I have a hunch it can't.

(Long pause.)

MICHAEL: The sun is cooling already.

PETER: The cold. *(Pause.)* Your coldness scares me.

MICHAEL: It protects me.

PETER: It shuts me out. *(Pause.)* I want to chip away
            at your coldness. Get rid of it. Get to the
            warmth.

MICHAEL: The layer is too thick.

PETER: I'll keep on trying.

MICHAEL: Be careful. Your chipping away might have
the opposite effect. It might just uncover an
even colder layer.

PETER: It's a risk.

MICHAEL: Even if it's so cold I freeze you out?

(They stare at each other.)

BLACKOUT

SCENE NINE

*(MICHAEL's flat. Evening. MICHAEL sitting on a chair
staring out at the audience. He is surrounded by a circle of
twelve tall, unlit candles. PETER enters with a lighted
birthday cake. There are twelve small candles on it.)*

PETER: *(Holding the cake out to MICHAEL.)* Blow
first. Your birthday cake.

MICHAEL: *(Looks at the candles on the cake, then slowly
blows them out. Pause.)* Twelve candles. I
didn't know I was that young.

PETER: For the months.

MICHAEL: I didn't think it was for the years we had
before us.

PETER: For the months we've had.

MICHAEL: We've had eleven months and sixteen days
together.

PETER: You've counted.

MICHAEL: *(Slowly.)* I count the days.

*(Takes the cake from PETER and places it on the floor.
Sits beside it.)*

PETER: *(After a long pause.)* Are you going to sit
there and <u>watch</u> it?

MICHAEL: Did you make it yourself?

PETER: You know I can't make cakes. The last time I tried I was at school. We had this cookery lesson and I nearly blew up the class. *(Awkward silence.)* Well, I thought it was funny.

MICHAEL: *(Quietly.)* The rest of the time we have together.

PETER: *(Kneels down in front of him.)* It'll be a long time.

MICHAEL: *(Looks sadly at him.)* Oh, and by what miracle? *(Pause.)* Are they going to develop the drug that will save us all tomorrow, or the day after tomorrow? Do you have information that I know nothing about?

PETER: *(Sits beside MICHAEL on the floor. He reaches out and touches the candles that surround them.)* No, I have no information.

MICHAEL: The candles add up to twelve. How many bloody more can there be?

PETER: We will add more.

MICHAEL: Six more? *(Pause.)* Or will we manage another twelve?

PETER: I am mentally adding years, not months.

(MICHAEL laughs. A cold laugh.)

PETER: Don't -

MICHAEL: It's my birthday.

PETER: Don't laugh like that.

MICHAEL: *(Pause.)* Will you give me an extra birthday present?

PETER: What?

MICHAEL: I want to play a game. A bit of role reversal.

PETER: Michael -

MICHAEL: All the best parties play games.

PETER: There are only the two of us.

MICHAEL: This _is_ a game for two. *(Pause.)* Later people from the BP group are coming. We couldn't play then.

PETER: *(Slowly.)* Do you want me to be here when they come? I know you said yes, and they agreed, but -

MICHAEL: I want you here. *(Takes PETER's hand.)* But in the meantime I want us to play out a scene.

PETER: *(Suspicious.)* Nothing morbid Michael.

MICHAEL: That's up to us not to make it so.

PETER: What do we do?

MICHAEL: I am you, and you are me. Let's light the candles again. Make it festive. Have you got matches?

PETER: *(Takes a lighter out of his pocket.)* I've got this.

MICHAEL: Then let's light them.

(PETER and MICHAEL light the tall candles. Minimal lighting in this scene until the game is over.)

PETER: So I'm you?

(They both stand, facing each other.)

MICHAEL: *(Emphatically.)* And I'm _you_.

(Long pause.)

PETER: This feels stupid. What do we do now?

MICHAEL: In as quiet, as cool a way as possible, we act out a goodbye scene. I want to see how we'd do it, me being you and you being me.

PETER: I won't do it.

MICHAEL: It's my extra birthday present remember?

(Long silence. PETER stares at MICHAEL warily.)

MICHAEL: Don't worry, it's not a death goodbye.

PETER: I still won't do it. *(Pause.)* I'm going to blow out the candles. The game's over.

MICHAEL: You'll ruin my birthday.

(MICHAEL grabs PETER's arm and prevents him from blowing out the candles. He twists PETER's arm painfully. PETER cries out.)

MICHAEL: We have gone to Paris for the weekend.

PETER: *(Almost crying.)* Not Paris. I want to go with you to Paris. I don't want us to go there to say goodbye.

MICHAEL: Late afternoon. A July 14 if you like. Lots of noisy tourists. Mostly English and German and American tourists, all clicking away with their cameras as they watch the parade go by. Such a party. *(Pause.)* Peter is bored with the crowds, and irritable. It's clear he's got something on his mind he wants to tell Michael. Michael suggests they go to a restaurant.

(MICHAEL picks up the cake and looks at it. PETER watches him.)

PETER: Are we still - ?

MICHAEL: Playing?

PETER: Yes.

MICHAEL: We are in the restaurant.

(MICHAEL kneels down on the floor with the cake and places it on the floor. He runs his fingers round the rim of the cake. Motions for PETER to join him on the floor.)

MICHAEL: This is a plate of very expensive food. I'm toying with my food.

PETER: *(Playing.)* What's wrong, Peter?

MICHAEL: I'm not hungry Michael. We've got to talk. I can't pretend any longer.

PETER: I don't understand.

MICHAEL: Michael, I want out.

PETER: *(Half playing.)* What?

MICHAEL: I thought I could. This afternoon I was going to tell you -

PETER: *(Panic creeping into his voice)* You thought you could what?

MICHAEL: Stand it, Michael. But I can't. *(Long pause.)* I can't watch what is happening to you and be unable to stop it. I want out. I want out before I get too involved.

PETER: *(No longer playing. Screams.)* I am too involved. I've been too involved for twelve months.

MICHAEL: *(Shouts.)* Play the game.

(Silence.)

MICHAEL: *(Shouts.)* Play.

PETER: No.

MICHAEL: *(Continuing to play.)* But Michael you have to understand that as much as I love you I'm not strong enough for it.

PETER: *(Screams violently.)* Stop.

(During MICHAEL's following speech PETER rushes round blowing out the candles.)

MICHAEL: *(Continuing.)* I'm scared I'll let you down when you do fall sick, and then I could never forgive myself for failing you. *(Pause.)* I know it's a shitty time to tell you this, but I can't keep quiet any longer. You need someone who is also HIV. You need someone who <u>really</u> understands. *(Pause.)* I just can't lie any longer. I'm weak. I want to get going before the going gets rough. I'm not as strong as you imagine.

(The stage lightens. PETER looks at MICHAEL. He is crying.)

PETER: I won't let you.

MICHAEL: Do what?

PETER: Use words I've never even thought of. *(Pause. Falls to the floor and while sobbing, hits it hard.)* I love you. How many times do I have to repeat it?

MICHAEL: *(Exhausted. His voice is quiet.)* Love. *(Pause.)* Peter think of some of the possible meanings. Here's one for you. *(Falls beside PETER and holds him tight. There is nothing gentle in this embrace.)* Love is giving what you haven't got to someone who just doesn't want it. *(Long pause.)* Now you can see how cold the layer underneath is.

BLACKOUT

SCENE TEN

(MICHAEL's flat. Night. Stage in semi-darkness. PETER has been waiting up for MICHAEL. He is lying down, half asleep and moving restlessly as if having a nightmare. MICHAEL enters. Full lights on. MICHAEL has been drinking. PETER starts, then shakes himself awake and gets up.)

MICHAEL: And before you say it, I had more than seven. *(Pause.)* Gin this time.

PETER: *(Quietly.)* I didn't ask.

MICHAEL: I've also had coffee. So don't make me coffee. *(Pause.)* What were you doing before you went to sleep? Reading?

PETER: TV. A late film.

MICHAEL: *(Not interested.)* What was it?

PETER: "The Dirty Dozen".

MICHAEL: Never seen it.

PETER: It wasn't very good.

MICHAEL: The title is lively.

(Long pause.)

PETER: Why?

MICHAEL: Don't go on. The sentence is too predictable. I drank because I felt like drinking. If we had a couple of cans in the house I'd continue drinking. *(Pause.)* And perhaps - just perhaps you'd join me.

PETER: There are a couple of lagers. Do you want me to get them?

MICHAEL: *(Mocking.)* Do you mean you'd actually drink with me?

PETER: If you like.

MICHAEL: It's no fun drinking with someone who does it
          for you.

PETER: I drink.

MICHAEL: Yes, but you don't drink.

PETER: Sorry.

MICHAEL: Maybe I'll drive you to it. *(Pause.)* You'd be
          ugly drunk. Might be worth it to see you ugly.
          At the moment I'd find a bit of rough ugliness
          attractive.

(PETER is silent. He rubs his face wearily.)

PETER: I'm tired.

MICHAEL: Then go to bed.

PETER: I'll call in sick tomorrow.

MICHAEL: Huh. Is that allowed - a healthy member of
          staff calling in sick at an Aids helpline?

PETER: *(Getting angry.)* You won't provoke me
          Michael.

MICHAEL: What sickness will you choose? A touch of
          flu? A bit of tummy trouble? Diarrhoea or
          constipation?

PETER: I'm going to bed.

MICHAEL: *(Quickly.)* Or sick because you are with me?

PETER: *(Trying to remain calm.)* I have headaches.
          Sinus trouble. You know that.

MICHAEL: Yes. I forgot. I always forget that you can be
          allowed to be genuinely ill. It's a selfish streak
          I have.

PETER: I'll ring in. *(Pause.)* We'll spend the day alone
          together. Go out to the cinema.

MICHAEL: No, thanks. The last time we did that, you took me to a re-run of "Night of the Living Dead". *(Pause.)* We don't have the same taste in - well, quite a few things really.

PETER: *(Quietly, after a long pause.)* Michael, do you want a row?

MICHAEL: Not particularly. The only thing in its favour is it might sober me up.

PETER: I'll get the cans.

MICHAEL: I'll have one if you have one.

PETER: A lager?

MICHAEL: No, a row.

PETER: I'll get the lagers.

(PETER exits. MICHAEL looks after him then kicks the side of the wall. PETER re-enters.)

MICHAEL: You saw that I suppose.

PETER: It's your wall.

MICHAEL: That's alright then, isn't it? I'm not damaging your property. You moved in with me - and when you're bored or tired or sick of me you can move out again.

(PETER opens a can. Hands it to MICHAEL.)

MICHAEL: You really drinking with me?

PETER: I have a can.

MICHAEL: You haven't opened it.

(PETER opens his can. Drinks.)

MICHAEL: Now lie and say you wanted it. Go on - *(Grabs PETER.)* - lie to me.

PETER: *(Pushes him away.)* Not funny, Michael.
             That's ugly.

MICHAEL: Well, aren't I?

PETER: No.

MICHAEL: I am ugly.

PETER: Stop it.

MICHAEL: I want to disgust you so that you'll stop.
             (Pause.) So that you'll stop wanting me.

(Silence.)

MICHAEL: Look.

PETER: I am looking.

MICHAEL: Look closely at my face.

(PETER looks. Long silence.)

MICHAEL: What do you see there?

PETER: The face of the person I -

MICHAEL: Don't say it again. Not love. Or care for. The
             reality, not that. *(Long pause. PETER says
             nothing.)* What do you see in my face?

PETER: I -

MICHAEL: You can see, but you can't say. Right? You
             can't even admit it to yourself. *(Pause.)* Look
             harder.

*(PETER looks. Then turns his face away. Stands with his
back to MICHAEL.)*

MICHAEL: I will tell you what you see if you really look.
             (Pause.) My hair is beginning to thin. I had
             beautiful hair a year ago. Real gay magazine
             stuff. But it's thinning now. It's not got much -
             how shall I put it? - advertising bounce to it.
             You couldn't sell shampoo with it.

PETER: *(Turning to face him.)* It's -

MICHAEL: Fading. The colour is fading. The texture is
            getting duller. *(Pause.)* Lifeless. That's the
            word. Lifeless hair. And then there's my skin.
            I have rashes a lot of the time, or hadn't you
            noticed?

PETER: I've noticed. *(Pause.)* Some people have a
            roughish skin.

MICHAEL: Mine was good. Until recently. Until the
            drugs. The drugs are saving my life, but they
            are not saving my skin. And being a shallow
            person, that makes me upset. I used to really
            get off on my skin.

PETER: You are being cruel to -

MICHAEL: You?

PETER: Yourself.

MICHAEL: My skin is being cruel to me. My hair is
            giving up on me. I've got nothing to do with it.
            (Long pause.) Of course there's positive
            thinking. I tried positive thinking. It makes
            you feel positive, except you end up
            wondering what exactly you are meant to feel
            positive about. *(Pause.)* I'd tell myself that
            with the right diet, the right sleep, the right
            health supplements - all the right things, that I
            would feel better about myself. And I did. I
            felt better feeling I should feel better. *(Pause.)*
            Then the night sweats, and the sallow skin,
            and the fading hair reminded me that inner
            well-bring is no real substitute for a rotting
            outer shell.

PETER: But it is only outer.

MICHAEL: Positive thinking couldn't help me with the fact - to me - that outer and inner are one and the same. *(Pause.)* I just can't stand the outside of me any more. And neither will you in time.

PETER: How can you say that and not want it to be different?

MICHAEL: *(Shouts.)* Of course I want it to be bloody different. I don't want to stay with you, and wait for you to catch up on my deterioration. I don't want the look in your eyes that says "ugh" when I open my mouth - and there inside my mouth you'll see a tongue covered in thrush. (Pause.) The sight that puts you off from kissing for life.

PETER: It's not that important.

MICHAEL: Isn't it? *(Pause.)* At the moment I'm proud of my muscles. My arms still look good. You've held them. You should know.

PETER: *(Beginning to cry.)* Why are you trying to drive me away? You don't want to. Not really. You love me, but you won't admit it.

MICHAEL: Counsellor talk.

PETER: *(Shouts.)* This is Peter, Michael, not a fucking counsellor. I'll stay up all night with you, but I'll get you to really talk to me.

MICHAEL: *(Quietly.)* Frank died tonight. I was at the hospital. We'd sat with him all day. During the afternoon he managed to talk. Plugged in, dripped in, with a catheter up his prick, he still managed to talk. *(Pause.)* "Get drunk guys, after I'm dead", he said, "do it for me. Piss me up to heaven." *(Long pause.)* I kept my promise. And here I am.

PETER: *(Gently.)* I'm glad you're here.

MICHAEL: Don't be tender.

PETER: I'm glad you're here. *(Pause.)* I can't bring
             Frank back. I can't help the hurting, not really.
             But I am here. *(Shouts at MICHAEL.)* Help
             me make that worth something.

BLACKOUT

SCENE ELEVEN

*(A counsellor's office. ERIC and PETER. Possible
suggestion for staging. A white screen. ERIC is behind the
screen in silhouette. PETER cannot focus on his face while
talking to him.)*

ERIC: Would you like something to drink? Coffee?
             Tea?

PETER: No, thanks.

ERIC: I'm afraid I have to tell you now that I have
             another person to see in half an hour.

PETER: Yes, I understand. It's good of you to take the
             time.

ERIC: I wish we weren't all so busy. I wish we had
             more time.

(Pause. ERIC is waiting for PETER to speak.)

PETER: I don't know where to begin. I'm not used to
             talking about myself to people I don't know.

ERIC: What about to the people you do know?

PETER: Depends. I've been called a fairly buttoned up
             type of man. I have this picture of myself
             trapped in buttons. Trapped in clothes. Even
             when I'm naked I don't really see myself

naked. *(Pause.)* I feel as if I'm with a
psychiatrist with you. I don't like the feeling.

ERIC: Have you ever seen a psychiatrist?

PETER: When I was nineteen, and I got cold feet about
           preferring men. *(Pause.)* In fact it wasn't men
           I had a fear of. It was Aids.

ERIC: Did the psychiatrist help the fear?

PETER: No.

ERIC: That's blunt enough.

PETER: He didn't help the fear, I did. I went out and
           slept with a guy. *(Pause.)* I chose the guy with
           care. I cruised the clubs and pubs until I found
           someone who had the courage to admit he was
           HIV.

ERIC: What happened when you returned to the
           psychiatrist?

PETER: I didn't return. I saw the guy I'd met, Simon,
           two or three times. Then through him I joined
           an Aids helpline. At first as a volunteer. Then
           when a job vacancy came up I went for it. I
           still have the job. As telephone receptionist.
           As typist.

ERIC: When you were with Simon, did the fear go
           away?

PETER: I think it just went inside. Now it's returned.
           (Pause.) I've fallen in love with a man who is
           HIV. Michael.

ERIC: What's the difference between Michael and
           Simon?

PETER: I told you. I'm in love with Michael. *(Pause.)* I
           wasn't with Simon. I didn't look at Simon and

fear that I'd lose him, and that there would be nothing left after that loss.

ERIC: And you do with Michael? *(PETER nods his head.)* Have you ever thought that you are deliberately putting yourself in situations that cause you pain?

PETER: I came here to talk with you. That sounds like jargon.

ERIC: I'm sorry if you think that.

PETER: That sounds like jargon too.

ERIC: I can't say what you want to hear.

PETER: How do you know what I want to hear?

ERIC: I'm trying to respond to what you have told me.

(Long pause.)

PETER: I don't want to see another psychiatrist.

ERIC: But you do need help. That's why you asked to see me.

PETER: I want to talk equally with someone. I don't want to be interpreted.

ERIC: I was suggesting a possible behaviour pattern.

(PETER paces the room.)

PETER: I have gone to bed with two men that I've known are HIV. I chose both of them for very different reasons. The first was to come to terms with a fear.

ERIC: There were other ways of dealing with that.

PETER: Like more therapy?

ERIC: Yes. More talking through the fears. Not necessarily with a professional.

PETER: *(Angrily.)* I wanted to act. I believe in action.

ERIC: Did you stop to think you were using this man Simon?

PETER: No, I didn't. He never gave me any reason to believe I was.

ERIC: Are you sure about that?

PETER: What you are saying is I am using Michael.

ERIC: I'm asking about this man Simon. *(Pause.)* You were dealing with someone vulnerable.

PETER: Because he's different as he's HIV?

ERIC: In a way - yes.

PETER: You make that sound unequal. It wasn't unequal. Simon and I talked about it. Michael and I talked and still talk about it. *(Pause.)* I didn't come here to feel guilty about sleeping with two men who are HIV.

ERIC: I know that.

PETER: You don't seem to. I feel as if I am being lectured, talked down to.

ERIC: That's not intended.

PETER: Why is it so wrong to have sex with a man who is antibody positive? Why do you, and other people, including some of those who are HIV, feel it is so wrong? Like a taboo?

ERIC: Possibly you get that impression because of their vulnerability. Sick people are more vulnerable than -

PETER: *(Shouts.)* Sick!

ERIC: The word makes you angry?

PETER: Too bloody right it does. Michael is not helped by a sick label. I am not helped by you telling me I am having sex with a sick label.

ERIC: Are you sure you are not HIV? Have you tested?

PETER: *(Coldly.)* Would that make it alright then if the test was positive? Would two vulnerable people be less of a threat?

ERIC: That's very hostile.

PETER: I feel hostile. I feel you are wanting "them" to be in one camp, and "us" - assuming I am not HIV - to be in another. Neat divisions. The age old different blood syndrome.

ERIC: I don't think you are using reason here.

PETER: How can I when all these reasons that people give me for my so-called behaviour are so primitive? *(Pause.)* It's all a question of blood in the end, isn't it? Keep the good blood away from the bad. The blacks had miscegenation in the South. They have it now in South Africa. We have it here with our classifications of infection and non-infection.

ERIC: *(Quietly.)* I thought you came here to talk about your fears.

PETER: It seems I am discovering new ones. Like just what I am up against with people like you. With certain people inside and outside of the helplines who want the divisions.

ERIC: You wouldn't be here if it wasn't causing problems.

PETER: True, but a lot of the problems could be dealt with if counsellors and others helped me live with Michael, not push me into leaving him.

ERIC: Are people honestly trying to do that?

PETER: There's nothing honest in it. There is nothing
            honest about one camp for the sick - your term
            - and the others. Others like me. And don't
            expect me to say healthy.

ERIC: I would like to help your anger.

PETER: *(Looking at his watch.)* Time is running out.

ERIC: The half hour isn't up, and anyway my next
            client can wait a bit. This is important.

PETER: For you?

ERIC: OK. We'll call this session over. But I'd like
            you to come back.

PETER: Yes. *(Pause.)* Thanks for asking.

BLACKOUT

SCENE TWELVE

*(MICHAEL's flat. MICHAEL is standing dressed in
pyjamas. His hair is slightly wet. The pyjamas are slightly
wet as well. He drinks some water. He sits down. Outside
in the street he hears two men shouting at each other. Most
of what they say is unintelligible, but the audience hears
clearly one of them say, "fuck off", and the second reply,
"piss off". PETER enters, naked. MICHAEL looks at him
and says nothing. Long silence.)*

PETER: What time is it?

MICHAEL: Four. Four-thirty.

PETER: The drunks are awake.

PETER: I heard them. *(Pause.)* What are you doing
            up?

PETER: I was worried about you.

MICHAEL: I've slept for over twelve hours. You shouldn't be worried about me. *(Pause.)* I didn't ask for anything.

PETER: I know, but all the same, I wanted to make sure. *(Pause.)* Does it still hurt?

MICHAEL: Yes.

PETER: Should you be drinking cold water? *(Pause.)* I could make you some soup.

MICHAEL: I didn't ask for anything.

PETER: Do you want me to go back to bed?

MICHAEL: This is nothing exceptional. You might as well.

PETER: But if you're in pain -

MICHAEL: I had a tooth out. I had two fillings. Of course I am in pain. I'm also not used to Valium.

PETER: Do you remember me putting you into bed yesterday afternoon?

MICHAEL: No. *(Pause.)* But thank you.

PETER: Maybe a little soup would do you some good.

MICHAEL: *(Exasperated.)* Peter, for Christ's sake -

(Long pause.)

PETER: I can't do it right, can I?

MICHAEL: This is no time to discuss -

PETER: *(Interrupting.)* I wanted to come to the dentist with you, but that woman -

MICHAEL: Carol.

PETER: Carol has a car. I haven't got a car. I earn a low wage remember, and I can't afford a car. Is it my fault if I can't afford a car? Is it my fault if we're both bloody poor? *(Long pause.)* I wanted to take you. We could have got a taxi.

MICHAEL: I've known Carol for a long time. She wanted to as well. It just seemed easier.

PETER: It made me feel useless.

MICHAEL: I think you're being selfish. I still feel dreadful. Can't this discussion wait?

(Long silence. Neither move.)

PETER: It hurt.

MICHAEL: *(Looking at him.)* You hurt!

PETER: Yes, I hurt. I wanted to be there.

MICHAEL: To hold my hand?

PETER: Just to be there.

MICHAEL: It may not have crossed your mind that I didn't want you sitting there, either holding my hand, or looking distressed about what was happening to me. *(Pause.)* Carol does neither. She's neutral.

PETER: I can't be neutral.

MICHAEL: If I wasn't HIV, would you still want to hold my hand at the dentist and make big cow eyes at me?

PETER: That's unkind. *(Pause.)* I wanted to show you I cared.

MICHAEL: You put me to bed when I came in. I can't remember it, but I'm grateful. That's enough to show me you care, but really I don't need constant proof, or for that matter you having to prove it to yourself.

PETER: *(Slowly.)* Where do I go wrong?

MICHAEL: For starters talking to me like this at some bloody ghastly hour of the morning after I've been butchered by the dentist.

PETER: I care.

MICHAEL: And you tell me you do, over and over again. You remind me all the time that I'm HIV by smothering me with attention. *(Pause.)* Oh, Peter, go to bed. It's no use this discussion. I'm tired. I'm not on form. We'll row. I don't need to row.

PETER: *(Suddenly shouts.)* I could fucking hit you at times.

MICHAEL: *(Quietly.)* Nice.

PETER: What am I supposed to do? Pretend you are alright?

MICHAEL: I am alright. And don't shout at me.

PETER: If I'm over protective, it's because I am scared.

MICHAEL: *(Slowly.)* Despite my reluctance to do so we'd better talk. *(Pause.)* Let me make one thing clear. You worrying, makes me worry. That doesn't do my immune system much good. I know you can't help but be worried, but it's a vicious circle. If you are over anxious that I might deteriorate or die on you that makes me even more conscious that I'm sick, and I don't want to feel that I'm sick.

PETER: Would someone who is HIV remind you less than I do?

MICHAEL: I haven't lived with someone who is HIV.

PETER: But would he have a different reaction?

MICHAEL: Well, whoever this hypothetical man is, I imagine he would have. Two people in the same boat tend to take it for granted they are in it together, and don't remind each other constantly of their situation.

PETER: And I am not in the same boat?

MICHAEL: Shall we drop the metaphors? At a quarter to five I prefer plain speaking. *(Pause.)* You are not to your knowledge HIV. *(Pause.)* I <u>am</u>. This makes you frightened of losing me to the great bogey man death, and makes you over anxious. Which frankly I can do without.

PETER: *(Reaches out for MICHAEL. Touches his hair. MICHAEL shrinks from his touch.)* You're wet.

MICHAEL: It's called a night sweat.

PETER: And your pyjamas are wet. Shall I get you a fresh pair?

MICHAEL: *(Shouts at him.)* No!

PETER: *(Calmly.)* It's probably the effect of the dentist. You feel as if you have a temperature.

MICHAEL: *(Takes off his pyjamas and stands naked in front of PETER.)* You have your wish. I need some clean pyjamas.

PETER: *(Shocked.)* You'll catch cold.

MICHAEL: *(Laughs.)* First I'm hot, then I'm going to catch cold. Why don't you rub me down with a towel? You like rubbing me down with a towel. It's one of those good, exciting things you like doing to me.

PETER: I'll get one. *(PETER leaves the room. MICHAEL stands motionless, waiting for PETER to return. Stares out at the audience. PETER returns with the towel.)*

PETER: You're shivering. Let me help you back to bed.

MICHAEL: *(Almost gently.)* It feels like torture what we are doing to each other.

PETER: The men outside said "fuck off" and "piss off" to each other. *(Pause.)* I don't want either of us to say that and to mean it.

MICHAEL: I know.

PETER: I can't - can't get it right all of the time. *(Pause.)* But at least let me try.

MICHAEL: *(Coldly. Like an order.)* Rub me down with the towel.

(PETER begins to rub him down.)

BLACKOUT

SCENE THIRTEEN

(A party. PETER on his own, slumped against a wall with a bottle in his hand. Music in background, also party noises. A MAN enters. PETER looks up at him. The MAN smiles. The MAN sits next to him, and leans with him against the wall.)

MAN: What a totally boring party. *(Turns to PETER.)* Why are you in the kitchen?

PETER: Everybody seems to be either in the main room, or the bedrooms. So I thought I'd come in here.

MAN: You should see the bedrooms. Or rather not see. Most of them are pitch black.

PETER: I have. *(Pause.)* Noisier than the music.

MAN: *(Laughs.)* Bloody stupid I call it.

PETER: What?

MAN: What's going on in them.

PETER: It's their business.

MAN: *(In a sing-song voice.)* The animals went in two by two...

PETER: *(Quickly.)* You're not going to compare us all to the ark are you? *(Pause.)* Spare us.

MAN: But isn't it? -

PETER: What?

MAN: Frightening?

PETER: *(Irritated.)* I think I know what you are talking about, and if you are you've picked the wrong man. I'm not even drunk enough to appreciate this conversation.

MAN: I want to talk to someone.

PETER: I want to drink. *(Drinks from the bottle.)* There's beer in the fridge if you want it.

MAN: I want to ask someone why they're taking all these risks.

PETER: Look I don't even know your name -

MAN: I mean in the upstairs bathroom two guys were lying on the floor, sucking each other off. *(Pause.)* With the light on!

PETER: Would it have been better if the light had been off?

MAN: You don't want to take this seriously.

PETER: As I said I don't know you from - *(Short pause.)* - no, I don't want to take this seriously. I came to this party so as to get away from taking things seriously. *(Pause.)* I admit it probably wasn't the right choice, but I came to not talk about what we're talking about.

MAN: Do you know people here?

PETER: Do you?

MAN: A friend's friend told me. He said they wouldn't be too fussy who they let in. The thought of the free drink was appealing. *(Pause.)* How did you know about it?

PETER: *(After a long pause.)* I work for an Aids helpline. A friend who works there gave me the address.

MAN: Is he here?

PETER: She, actually. *(Pause.)* No, she's not here.

(Uncomfortable silence.)

MAN: Why do you do that?

PETER: What?

MAN: Work for them?

PETER: Who are "them"?

MAN: Aids people.

PETER: This is none of your business.

MAN: No need to get rude. *(Pause.)* The last person I want to end up with is a guy who has got the virus.

PETER: I wish I was drunk so as I could not understand this conversation.

MAN: Well, what do you think about it?

(PETER stands up.)

PETER: I should be getting home.

MAN:	*(An aggressive note in his voice.)* Pushing off then?
PETER:	It's late.
MAN:	Have you got it?

(PETER stares down at him. He doesn't answer immediately. He is too angry.)

PETER:	I'm not answering that.
MAN:	You should. *(Slight pause.)* I've been tested.
PETER:	That was your decision.
MAN:	You mean you work with them, and you don't all get tested? That's bloody outrageous.
PETER:	That's a matter of opinion. *(Pause.)* I don't want to go into the opinions on the subject.
MAN:	I've tested every six months since the thing started. I come out negative each time. I intend to stay that way.
PETER:	It's your choice to test.
MAN:	You sound like those counsellors. Are you?
PETER:	I'm a receptionist. *(Pause.)* Now can I go politely?
MAN:	Wait - hold on. Don't be angry. I'm not getting at you. Sit down with me again. Please. *(Pause.)* Can I have some of your beer?
PETER:	The fridge is -
MAN:	Yours will do.
PETER:	My lips have touched the bottle.
MAN:	I wasn't saying you've got it. And I know you can't get it that way.
PETER:	*(Hands him the bottle.)* It's tepid by now.

MAN: *(Wipes the rim of the bottle with the sleeve of his shirt.)* It's wet. *(Drinks. Hands the bottle back to PETER.)* Anyway I can see you've not got it. You're not thin.

PETER: *(Sits down again next to the MAN. Looks at him, then asks quietly.)* Do you really believe that? That you can tell by looking that someone is HIV?

MAN: I know it's bloody invisible.

PETER: You're really scared, aren't you?

MAN: Too right I am. *(Pause.)* My last boyfriend. I suspected he was sleeping around. I chucked him at once. Supposing he had caught it?

PETER: Supposing he had?

MAN: It would have been his own fault. I blame the lot of them that get it. Oh, I know you probably feel sorry for them, and feel it's a good cause working for them, but you can't deny they put themselves at risk.

PETER: *(Slowly.)* I happen to be in love with someone who has got "it" as you call it.

(Long silence.)

MAN: Why?

PETER: Why what?

MAN: Why love him? There are plenty of healthy people left to choose from.

(PETER looks at the man in silence. Too shocked to answer.)

MAN: Did you know he had it when you met him?

PETER: From the first meeting. Yes.

MAN: That's sick.

PETER: I don't want to get angry with you. I know you
           are scared.

MAN: Don't be patronising. I feel angry because a
           nice looking man like you could put himself at
           risk.

PETER: *(Patiently.)* My lover is not a risk.

MAN: Do you - ?

PETER: Do we fuck? I presume that's what you want
           to ask. *(Pause.)* We make love. We do that.
           We also take precautions.

MAN: It's sick. I'm not alone in feeling that. Most of
           my friends wouldn't go near a guy who is
           HIV.

PETER: Really.

MAN: No, they wouldn't.

PETER: I expect a few of them are HIV themselves.

MAN: Then I expect they have sex with their own
           kind. They certainly don't boast about it.

PETER: If I stay a minute longer with you I am going
           to revert to savagery. I am going to smash
           your ignorant foul mouth in. *(Stands up and
           looks down at the man.)* Have a nice end of
           party. *(He exits.)*

BLACKOUT

SCENE FOURTEEN

*(MICHAEL's flat. PETER is running from one side of the
room to the other, hitting the walls with his hands as he
does so. He does this for as many times as the actor feels is
necessary to convey panic and anger. MICHAEL is seated
at the front of the stage reading a book. Eventually PETER*

stops hitting the walls and goes to stand behind
MICHAEL. He looks over his shoulder.)

PETER: Good book?

MICHAEL: Mmm.

PETER: *(Trying to suppress his anger.)* You've been
            reading it for an hour.

MICHAEL: Mmm.

PETER: The story must be compelling.

MICHAEL: Mmm.

PETER: Why do you always say "mmm"?

MICHAEL: Mmm.

PETER: I suppose that's an answer.

*(PETER suddenly takes the book out of MICHAEL's hand
and throws it on the floor.)*

MICHAEL: *(Coldly.)* That was unpleasant.

PETER: So is talking to myself for hours when I'm
            supposed to be talking to you.

MICHAEL: *(Stands. Faces him.)* Supposed? I don't know
            that I'm supposed to do anything with anyone.

PETER: We had a meal. You said practically nothing.
            (Pause.) Sorry, you asked me to pass the salt.

MICHAEL: Which isn't good for me.

PETER: You asked me to pass the salt. I don't believe
            you said another word to me.

MICHAEL: I said the salad dressing tasted too sharp.

PETER: *(Sarcastically.)* Did you? In the silence I
            didn't hear.

MICHAEL: I had nothing to say.

PETER: You are not talking to me. Not tonight. Not
            the night before. *(Pause.)* I didn't see you the
            night before that. So if I calculate right, we
            have not talked in about four days.

MICHAEL: I have nothing to say.

PETER: Then why have me around?

MICHAEL: You have moved in with me. *(Pause.)* It
            wouldn't be polite to ask you to go.

PETER: No, it wouldn't be polite. *(Pause.)* But I will
            go. *(PETER moves to exit. MICHAEL shouts
            after him and in doing so prevents him from
            going.)*

MICHAEL: *(Stands.)* Sometimes I need solitude.

*(Both move closer together. The next three lines are
shouted at each other.)*

PETER: For four days when you're living with
            someone?

MICHAEL: Four, five, do we have to count?

PETER: We haven't even a dog I can take for a walk.

(Silence.)

MICHAEL: *(Quietly.)* You've made your point. I've shut
            you out.

PETER: *(Questioning.)* Yes?

MICHAEL: You're right.

PETER: Why?

(Long pause.)

MICHAEL: Five nights ago you did something -

PETER: I did a lot of things five nights ago.
            (Flippantly.) I had some beers. I've become
            quite an alcoholic. You had some beers with

me. I think we got rather drunk if I can
remember.

MICHAEL: *(Shouts.)* Yes, trying to forget that I'm HIV
and that you are not.

(Silence.)

MICHAEL: *(Quieter.)* No, I'm thinking of something else.
I am thinking of something <u>painfully</u> specific.

*(Pause. MICHAEL stares hard at PETER when he says
"painfully". PETER knows what he is talking about.)*

PETER: I understand.

MICHAEL: It was - *(Long pause.)* - I don't have the
words.

PETER: I wanted you.

MICHAEL: You could have restrained yourself.

PETER: *(Angrily.)* It was my decision.

MICHAEL: Since when is it one person's decision to turn
the person they're having sex with...

PETER: *(Interrupts.)* ...making love to...

MICHAEL: ...having sex with into a potential killer? If not
physically, then psychologically. *(Pause.)* Did
you stop to think of the damage it caused me?

PETER: The chances are –

MICHAEL: *(Shouts.)* Real! *(Pause.)* It was dangerous.
And you have no excuse.

PETER: I -

MICHAEL: No excuse. You wanted my arse. You wanted
to put your cock up my arse and that's all there
was to it.

PETER: I didn't do it.

MICHAEL: No. I made my decision, remember? I wasn't willing to let you do a re-run of "Death Wish". *(Pause.)* You do like trashy films don't you?

PETER: Shut up Michael.

MICHAEL: You wanted to talk. I'm now in the mood to reply.

PETER: *(Slowly.)* I - I do not have a death wish. I love you, even though you never tell me you love me.

MICHAEL: I think we're changing the subject now.

PETER: No, we are very much with the subject. I don't want your death, I don't want my death.

MICHAEL: Then understand that I care about you enough not to want to put you at risk.

PETER: Care. Not love. You never say love.

MICHAEL: *(Avoiding this.)* But you obviously do not care enough about me to avoid putting me into an embarrassing, cruel situation. *(Bends down and picks up the book.)*

PETER: Don't for fuck's sake start reading again.

MICHAEL: I want to see how chapter four ends.

PETER: Put it down.

MICHAEL: Maybe it has a bad ending.

PETER: *(Angrily snatches the book from MICHAEL's hand.)* I'll tell you. *(Flicks through the pages.)* Last sentence of chapter four: "Mrs Austen clearly felt that she had had enough of these crises, and one can hardly blame her." *(Looks at the cover.)* "The Double Life of Jane Austen". *(Puts book down.)*

MICHAEL: I like to read about Jane Austen.

PETER: Does this book imply she had a more exciting
            life than we know about?

MICHAEL: At least she was polite. And had manners.

PETER: She also wasn't HIV.

MICHAEL: Sod you. *(Long silence. There is a moment
            when MICHAEL could either beat PETER up
            or cry. MICHAEL begins to cry.)*

PETER: *(Gently.)* Don't. Don't cry.

MICHAEL: I want you to go.

PETER: I know you do.

*(PETER sits down on the floor. MICHAEL stops crying.
There is no emotion in MICHAEL's voice.)*

MICHAEL: I said I want you to go.

PETER: *(Shakes his head slowly.)* I don't understand.
            Why do tears upset me? Why do your tears
            upset me?

MICHAEL: *(Looks at him.)* What?

PETER: Why can't I bear to see you cry? *(Pause.)* I
            love you, and I can't bear to see you cry.

MICHAEL: I don't think we should talk any more.

PETER: I get to know new things about you every day.
            I didn't know you liked Jane Austen. *(Pause.)*
            There is so much I don't know about you.

MICHAEL: Maybe the HIV gets in the way of finding out.

PETER: *(Quietly.)* Yes, maybe it does. *(Long pause.)*
            Do you want to know what happened five
            nights ago?

*(MICHAEL picks up book. Opens it and sits down on the
floor at a distance from PETER. He looks at a page, but is
obviously not reading.)*

PETER: What happened was I forgot you were HIV.

(MICHAEL looks up slowly from the page.)

PETER: I forgot. I behaved as if there were no barriers
            there. The feeling of love was so great I didn't
            think of protection. I behaved as we once all
            used to behave, spontaneously. *(Pause.)* I
            didn't make any decision about it.

MICHAEL: *(Puts down book.)* I - I don't know what to
            say.

PETER: Even during the past few days, the shutting
            me out, I didn't think I had done wrong.
            (Pause.) Tonight, rightly, you made me
            remember.

MICHAEL: *(Gets up and crosses over to PETER. Sits
            down beside him.)* It's such a mess, isn't it?

PETER: *(Shakes his head. Almost laughs.)* No. No, it's
            simple. *(He takes MICHAEL's hand and
            strokes it.)* We can't avoid every risk.

MICHAEL: *(Almost inaudibly.)* I know. *(Looks at PETER
            for a long while.)* I - I love you. I love you so
            very much.

*(MICHAEL kisses PETER passionately on the mouth, then
draws him to him.)*

MICHAEL: Hold me. I feel cold. Suddenly I feel cold. I
            need your warmth.

BLACKOUT

END OF PLAY

FREEDOM TO PARTY

Characters

MARK, early forties
SIMON, early forties.
ALEX, a few years older than MARK, but looks younger.
PAUL, mid-twenties.

Place

The place is MARK's house. A place of memory, place of mirrors. Broken glass in the walls and on the floor. Furniture only when needed. Remnants of an old party remain, perhaps a few champagne bottles. Basic image of mirrors, glass and bottles.

Time

Sometime in the 21st Century.

SCENE ONE

(Stage in total Darkness. Voices heard in darkness. This scene may, alternatively, be staged under harsh lighting in which case the director should find the appropriate images of violence.)

MAN 1: Are you queer?

MAN 2: He's queer.

MAN 3: Do you fuck it or suck it?

MAN 2: He's a fucking queer. So let him suck it.

(Laughter.)

MAN 2: Speak up then queer. Tell us what you prefer.

PAUL: Leave me alone.

MAN 2: Leave me alone, he says. Shall we leave him alone?

(Laughter.)

MAN 1: No.

MAN 3: Sod the bastard.

MAN 1: Bugger the sod.

MAN 2: No, he might have a new disease. 'bout time they found a new one. The queers. *(Pause.)* Remember Aids?

MAN 1: Yeah, son of Aids!

MAN 3: Give it to the bastard. Give it to him, Phil.

MAN 2: Want it then? Go on - talk.

PAUL: No.

MAN 2: What?

PAUL: No.

MAN 2: Louder.

PAUL: No.

MAN 1: He meant yes. Did you all hear him say yes? Son of Aids said yes.

MAN 3: Give it to him then. Show him what you've got, Phil.

MAN 1: He's got a big one.

MAN 3: Yeah.

MAN 1: Shove it up his nothing cunt.

MAN 3: A thick icy big one. Give it to him, Phil.

MAN 1: Say yes to the knife, son of Aids. Say you want it.

PAUL: No.

MAN 1:   He's seen it, Phil. He's real scared now.

MAN 2:   Say you want it queer.

MAN 1:   Up his big O. Up his big cunt.

MAN 2:   Go on say it.

PAUL: No. Leave me alone.

(Voices begin to chant 'CUNT, CUNT, CUNT, CUNT.....'.)

(Cut to silence.)

SCENE TWO

(Stage in darkness. Sound of loud hammering on the door. This sound rises to a crescendo, then subsides. Lights up. Bright lights. PAUL is seated on a chair facing the audience. MARK stands behind him, bending over his face. PAUL's face is bleeding, and when MARK applies cotton wool to it, he screams.)

MARK: *(Quietly.)* Be quiet. It'll be alright. Be quiet.

PAUL: The bastards -

MARK: I know.

PAUL: *(Twisting away.)* What do you know? It's never
          happened to you.

MARK: A lot of things have happened to me that you
          don't know about. *(Dabs again. PAUL cries out
          again.)* Be quiet. How can I help you if you
          won't let me?

PAUL: You are making it worse.

MARK: *(Draws back.)* Do you want me to take you to the
          hospital, and let them deal with it?

PAUL: No.

MARK: We can. Car's outside. *(Pause.)* I think it's only a small cut. There's lots of blood because they caught the flesh under the eye.

PAUL: The knife was long and sharp. *(Pause.)* It hurts like hell, and you're making it hurt more.

MARK: I'm sorry. Perhaps you'd better do it yourself.

PAUL: You think I'm a coward, don't you?

MARK: I think you've had a fright and a superficial wound.

PAUL: *(Gets up. Looks into a mirror.)* They nearly got my eye.

MARK: They didn't.

PAUL: They nearly got my eye. I could have lost my sight. *(Takes the cotton wool from MARK's hand and dabs at the wound himself.)*

MARK: Hurt as much when you do it?

PAUL: *(Dabs again.)* Can you get me some water?

(MARK exits. PAUL steps back and stares at his reflection in the mirror. He raises a fist as if to strike the image there. MARK returns with a bowl of water. He sees the gesture.)

PAUL: *(Still staring into the mirror.)* I'll be twenty-five next month. Youth gone. This wound if it had been worse would have really done me in.

MARK: Don't exaggerate.

PAUL: *(Dabs cotton wool in water, then wipes at his face.)* You were never afraid of growing old I suppose? *(Steps back from mirror.)* That's better. You're right, the wound is small. We got any plaster?

MARK: In the bathroom.

(PAUL leaves the room. MARK buries his face in his hands. PAUL is back very quickly. Sees him.)

PAUL: You alright?

MARK: A headache.

PAUL: You should feel mine. I'm the one who got bashed.

MARK: It's late, and it was a shock for me too. It sounded like all hell had broken loose. *(Pause.)* Like the Police had come. I used to dream about the Police when I was your age - beating down the doors. *(Changes the subject.)* Have you got the plaster?

PAUL: Yes.

MARK: Better put it on, in case you start bleeding again. *(Pause.)* Go on. Do it.

PAUL: *(Looks in the mirror as he puts on the plaster.)* I never liked the look of blood. I don't like the colour red much. When they ganged up on me I thought, 'Oh God, they're gonna make me all red'. Silly the things that go through your head when you're in danger.

MARK: *(Smiles.)* Yes.

PAUL: I mean they could have killed me.

MARK: *(Gently.)* What happened?

PAUL: *(Turns away from the mirror. Sits down. Speaks slowly.)* We were in the usual pub. There was a disco at the back. I know it's a mistake to go there Saturday nights, as that's when they usually get trouble - but you know I like mixed pubs, and I was feeling reckless. *(Pause.)* I was with Tom and a few other people you don't know.

MARK: *(Interrupting.)* Most of your friends I don't know.

PAUL: Then this group of three, maybe four, I can't remember, came out of the disco area, and they saw Tom with his arm around my shoulder. *(Pause.)* We looked..... intimate.

MARK: *(Quietly.)* I see.

PAUL: We looked intimate, and they started calling us names. They called me a male cunt, and the others with us left, and I told Tom to go.

MARK: Why didn't you go with him?

PAUL: 'cos then they would have got Tom as well. They singled me out as soon as they saw me. A small group of guys always choose one or two at the most. *(Pause.)* They wanted me, and I didn't want them to get Tom.

MARK: Noble.

PAUL: *(Angrily.)* Don't knock it. *(Pause.)* I thought alone I could talk them out of violence, but they really wanted me. *(Pause.)* The staff were useless. Too scared they'd have their bottles smashed up. Even the fucking Doberman they have for protection did a bunk.

MARK: And?

PAUL: They told me to go out into the street. I said no, and they dragged me out. The staff and the others pretended not to notice. Outside in the street they touched me. They taunted me. One of them had a knife. The guy with the knife said, 'Remember Aids?'

MARK: *(Surprised.)* What?

PAUL: You heard. He said, 'Remember Aids?'

MARK: *(Slowly.)* Why?

PAUL: If you went out more often, you'd know it's a common taunt. Like sons of Aids. Guys of our age get called that too. *(Quickly.)* This isn't the first time I've been attacked. I've been hit before, but there's never been a knife before. I was scared of that. Scared of disfigurement. *(Pause.)* We all look good now. I don't want to look different. I don't want to look as if I've been through anything.

(Long silence.)

MARK: I'm sorry. I really am sorry.

PAUL: Want to give me a drink?

MARK: Brandy? A whisky? What do you want?

PAUL: I want a drink. Any drink. A beer.

MARK: Sure it's a beer?

PAUL: Two if we've got them.

MARK: I'll go and see. *(MARK goes off stage, gets beers, then returns.)*

PAUL: *(Takes the beer from him. Long pause. Drinks slowly. Looks up at MARK.)* There was a call for you. Before I went out. You were in the bath.

MARK: Did you take a message?

PAUL: Yeah. He said he'd ring back.

MARK: Well, it probably wasn't important.

PAUL: There were background noises. Sounded long distance. *(Short pause.)* The name was English. Alan. Yes, I think it was Alan.

MARK: I don't know any Alans.

PAUL: Something like that. *(Irritably.)* Is this a time for me to remember? *(Pause.)* Yeah, I do remember. It was Alex.

(Long silence. MARK is visibly surprised. He sits down.)

PAUL: Bad news?

MARK: Alex...are you sure?

PAUL: I think it was Alex.

MARK: *(Slowly.)* What - what did he say?

PAUL: He said, 'Tell Mark I'll call again later'.

MARK: How much later? What did he say?

PAUL: I didn't ask.

MARK: *(Long pause.)* It could be -

PAUL: Who?

MARK: It could be someone I haven't heard from in years.

PAUL: Oh. That sort of call.

MARK: I'm not sure what you mean.

PAUL: An old lover? *(Looks at MARK. Pause. Awkward silence.)* Well, no doubt he will call again.

MARK: *(Quietly.)* Yes.

PAUL: Look, I'm bored with the subject already. I'm bruised and hurt, and this water needs throwing out. It's red with blood.

(PAUL exits. MARK stares after him.)

BLACKOUT

SCENE THREE

(A week later. MARK & SIMON. MARK has just finished a phone call. SIMON is staring at him intently. MARK takes a long time to speak.)

SIMON: *(Slowly.)* Is it who I think it is?

MARK: Yes.

SIMON: I hope you did the right thing.

MARK: He took a week to ring back. *(Pause.)* Do you think he has changed?

SIMON: Well, I look in the mirror and I'm not twenty, or whatever it was anymore. Time must have left its traces, even for Alex.

MARK: I used to wish he'd get fat and ugly.

SIMON: *(Smiling.)* He probably has. He's probably got a beer gut that hangs over a pair of jeans that are far too tight for him. You'll take one look and wonder - *(Stops.)*

MARK: Yes?

SIMON: Nothing.

MARK: No, go on. You wanted to say something else. *(Pause.)* I want you to say it.

SIMON: It's all water under the bridge.

MARK: The water is running backwards now. So you might as well finish what you wanted to say.

SIMON: It wasn't very nice, what I was going to say.

MARK: I didn't think it was. But maybe I need to hear it. We are survivors, remember? I need to know what you think.

SIMON: OK. You'll take one look at him and wonder how he could have done what he did. *(Pause.)* You won't see the beer gut or the awful clothes.

MARK: He may have a trim figure and be stunning.

SIMON: *(Slowly.)* Could he still - well, stun you?

(PAUL enters. Looks uncertainly at the two.)

PAUL: Am I disturbing anything?

MARK: Simon and I were talking about old times.

PAUL: Fascinating. When don't you?

SIMON: I don't come around often Paul, when I know you are here.

MARK: Simon, don't -

SIMON: Sorry Paul. No offence. I'm like that with all young people. Been around too long.

PAUL: *(Ignoring him.)* Mark I need a clean shirt. Can I borrow one of yours?

MARK: Of course.

PAUL: Thought I'd ask. Now I'll leave you to whatever interesting bits of personal history you were raking over.

SIMON: I've got to go in a minute.

PAUL: Stay and keep Mark company. I'll be gone all evening. The drinks will go on forever, then I'll forget the time, and as usual roll in drunk at around four in the morning. *(Pause.)* Mark constantly urges me to go out and mix with my own age group, so don't think I'm treating him badly.

SIMON: I wasn't thinking.

PAUL: You have that stern, army officer look on your face.

SIMON: I was never an army officer.

PAUL: Pity. It's so disciplinary. *(Pause.)* Masculine.

SIMON: *(Slowly.)* I'm a chemist, remember?

PAUL: I'll stick with the army. It excites my fantasies more. But then, that's assuming that I find you attractive, and I don't. *(Turns to Mark.)* I'll borrow your blue shirt.

MARK: *(Quietly.)* Alright.

PAUL: *(Kisses him.)* You look gloomy. Tired?

SIMON: He's had a hard day at work too.

PAUL: Of course. The boss is tired. I'm selfish. *(Kisses Mark again.)* Love you though. *(Exits.)*

SIMON: Why - ?

MARK: Why do I put up with him?

SIMON: Well, why do you?

MARK: I love him.

SIMON: You have practically nothing in common.

MARK: Wrong. *(Pause.)* He keeps me in touch with what's going on out there. The new trends and tastes. It's vital if our channel is going to stay on top. I trust his judgement.

SIMON: I wouldn't. No wonder your "Lifestyle" channel has got so boring over the last couple of years.

MARK: Stop it, Simon. Don't keep knocking him. *(Pause.)* He has a lot to cope with, living with me. *(Looks at SIMON.)* Was I ever easy?

SIMON: No, but you deserve better than him.

MARK: We choose what we want.

SIMON: He reminds me of Alex when he was his age.

MARK: I know.

SIMON: The way he flaunts about and struts. Alex was like that.

MARK: Yes.

SIMON: Am I opening wounds?

MARK: Not as much as when I come face to face with Alex again. But you know Simon, Paul isn't anything like him. Alex was - well, genuinely more selfish. He didn't care, deep down he didn't care. The mask peeled off to reveal another mask, and then when you peeled that another mask. I still want to know who the real Alex was. *(Pause.)* Is.

SIMON: Paul's got a mask too.

MARK: Yes, but underneath he is - *(Pause.)* - there.

SIMON: I'm not convinced.

MARK: You don't like him.

SIMON: True, but I think he's closer to how Alex was than you care to admit.

MARK: Let's have a drink. I feel like getting rather drunk tonight.

SIMON: I'm willing.

MARK: Do you remember - *(Goes off stage.)*

SIMON: *(Calls after him.)* What?

MARK: *(Returning.)* Do you remember how we gave up drink, and poppers and cigarettes, and sex?

SIMON: No, I didn't give up sex.....or cigarettes.

MARK: *(Laughing.)* You told me you had.

SIMON: Said that to make you feel better. Solidarity with the spirit of the thing. And oh boy were you into the spirit of the thing. *(Pause. Imitates MARK.)* I'm HIV and I won't touch anyone. *(Smiles.)* That was your motto.

MARK: Wasn't as simple as that.

SIMON: Too right it wasn't. Not for me anyway. I used condoms as quickly as I got through cigarettes.

MARK: *(Laughs.)* We've never discussed those days much, have we?

SIMON: I'm not one for memory lane.

MARK: *(Quietly.)* Survivors.

SIMON: So?

MARK: Funny feeling.

SIMON: We survived the survival. We've never needed to talk about it. We both had the disease. *(Pause.)* We went through it together, remember?

(Silence.)

MARK: *(Slowly.)* I really believed I was going to die. Do you know that?

SIMON: *(Gently.)* I know that.

MARK: No wonder we don't talk about it. It was awful.

SIMON: I whistled in the dark. I put on the clown's mask.

MARK: And here we are - alive.

SIMON: Don't regret it. We'll die soon enough. The reprieve wasn't meant to last forever.

MARK: But the drugs that saved us made us immortal - at the time. *(Quickly.)* Come on, drink your drink. I want to get drunk mutually.

SIMON: As I said, I'm willing. Top me up. And you'd better get another bottle.

MARK: I'll get the bottle.

(MARK exits. Sound of breaking glass. MARK cries out. SIMON rushes off stage. MARK continues crying. SIMON returns, almost carrying MARK.)

MARK: *(Shaking.)* Glass everywhere.

SIMON: Don't worry about that. I'll clean up.

MARK: Last bottle.

SIMON: I'll go out and buy another.

MARK: I can't stop shaking.

SIMON: Lie down.

MARK: Hold me. Close.

(SIMON holds MARK. MARK kisses SIMON suddenly on the mouth. SIMON leans his head back and looks at MARK in surprise.)

MARK: I love you Simon.

SIMON: *(Hopeful surprise in his voice.)* Love you too.

MARK: As friends.

SIMON: *(Disappointed.)* Of course.

MARK: Did me good.

SIMON: *(Flatly.)* Friendly kisses are good.

MARK: *(Slowly.)* I dropped the bottle. I saw something.

SIMON: What?

MARK: *(Shudders.)* Me and Alex. Twenty years ago. I suddenly saw us as we were.

SIMON: And?

MARK: I saw us in bed together. It was the last night before he left. *(Pause.)* I reached out and touched him. I tried to kiss him, and he crawled away from me to the farthest corner of the bed. I lay on my side of the bed for the rest of the night feeling dirty, as if I had committed a dirty act.

SIMON: *(Caressing MARK.)* He was scared.

MARK: He was disgusted by me.

SIMON: Did he say that?

MARK: He didn't say anything. *(Long pause.)* The next day he was gone.

SIMON: I remember.

MARK: But I haven't told you the rest. In that bed, before I touched him, I told him how afraid I was. I told him how the doctors were going to put me on to stronger drugs. I told him I thought I would die. *(Pause.)* I even asked him not to leave me. I begged him in the darkness not to leave me. *(Pause.)* He didn't say anything. It was like he was dead beside me.

SIMON: Did you really beg?

MARK: I saw myself dying alone. The image was awful. I wanted assurance. I wanted him to assure me he would be there, with me, right up until the last. *(Pause.)* I wasn't the kind who wants to die alone.

SIMON: *(Slowly.)* I would have been there.

MARK: Yes - but I wanted him. *(Screams.)* I wanted him. I wanted him like I want Paul now. But I'll never make that mistake again. I'll never beg again. *(Pause.)* And Paul's scared of death. Like Alex. Oh yes, they're alike on that. *(Pause.)* He'd walk out on me, do you know that, if he knew I had

had Aids? He hates Aids, and sometimes I feel he is so scared of what happened to us then, that he hates those who died. *(Pause.)* Any mention of our history, of what happened to people like you and I, would turn the party he's trying to have into a screaming nightmare. To survive they have to forget us. *(Slowly.)* Who is to say Aids, or something like that won't return? They know that. I know that. He can't take on that past. And he gets beaten up, even now, for what happened to us then.

SIMON: I know he doesn't know about me.

MARK: *(Takes SIMON's hand.)* I'm scared. Alex is coming back. *(Pause.)* I'm scared.

SIMON: I'll be there.

BLACKOUT

SCENE FOUR

(Stage in darkness. Loud hammering on the door. Lights. Bright lights. MARK and PAUL naked on the bed. MARK jerks up, crying out. He gets up from the bed. Stands shivering.)

MARK: Did you hear it?

PAUL: *(Sleepily.)* What?

MARK: The hammering. The noise.

PAUL: *(Gets up.)* A nightmare. *(Tries to pull MARK back down onto the bed.)* Come back. Lie down.

MARK: *(Struggling.)* It was real.

PAUL: It was a nightmare.

MARK: It was real. It is real. They are at the door.

PAUL: Nonsense. Lie down. It was a bad dream. Come
        on, you are waking me up.

MARK: I'm scared.

PAUL: Shhh.

MARK: I'm scared.

PAUL: Come on! I'm up early today, remember? Got
        that new show, remember? A lot of work to do.

MARK: They are there.

PAUL: *(Forcibly pulls MARK back down on to the bed.
        Pins MARK down with his own body. Shouts
        down at him.)* There is no one at the door. I'll
        open it to show you.

MARK: *(Still struggling.)* No. Stay with me. Don't leave
        me.

PAUL: Keep still. *(Pause. MARK relaxes, and PAUL
        falls away from him.)* Go back to sleep.

MARK: Yes.

PAUL: No more nonsense?

MARK: No more nonsense. *(Begins to cry.)* Stay with
        me.

PAUL: Shhh. Go to sleep.

BLACKOUT

SCENE FIVE

*(The following morning. MARK gets out of bed first, and
sits for a while looking at PAUL asleep. He reaches out
and strokes his hair, then as PAUL begins to waken he
shakes him gently.)*

MARK: Coffee?

PAUL: *(Trying to go back to sleep.)* No.

MARK: You are not going back to sleep.

PAUL: *(Sits up.)* I got a rotten night's sleep.

MARK: I know. I'm sorry.

PAUL: Why don't you take pills if it's getting this bad?

MARK: I do take pills.

PAUL: These dreams. Most nights. You hear things. See things.

(PAUL gets up. Dresses. MARK watches him, then puts on his clothes as well.)

MARK: Why do you always make me feel I disturb your sleep on purpose?

PAUL: I just need sleep.

MARK: And I said I'm sorry. I can't stop the dreams because you need them to stop.

PAUL: Maybe we should start sleeping in separate rooms.

MARK: Do you want that?

(Silence.)

PAUL: *(Slowly.)* I'll go and make the coffee.

MARK: I want you to answer that.

PAUL: I can't. I don't know.

MARK: After four years I can't imagine spending a night without you.

PAUL: *(Embarrassed.)* No, well...

MARK: But you can?

PAUL: I didn't say that.

MARK: It doesn't really matter to you does it being beside me? It doesn't count.

PAUL: Not in the same way it does for you. *(Pause.)* I want to be there, but I need my night's sleep undisturbed. *(Pause.)* Anyway, why are the nights so bad?

MARK: *(Shakes his head slowly.)* I can't say.

PAUL: You must have some idea.

MARK: Memories. I remember things. I re-live things.

PAUL: Like the Police hammering on the door?

MARK: *(Slowly.)* When I was younger I was afraid of them. I imagined they'd come and drag me away.

PAUL: *(Laughs.)* Why in hell?

MARK: They were bad days.

PAUL: I know, but the bad things happened to other people. You were in your own business. It didn't affect you personally.

MARK: Everything around me affected me personally. I was disturbed by it.

PAUL: Does it mean you've got to re-live all those things in your sleep?

MARK: *(Slowly.)* Why are you so callous Paul? I just don't understand why you think all of that is in the past. The other night. What happened to you. It's better now, but it's still bad.

PAUL: It's not as bad as you'd like to think tucked up here. You're so out of touch. *(Pause.)* We have fun out there you know.

MARK: But behind the fun are - *(Searches for the word.)* - shadows.

PAUL: Shadows most of us don't want. And don't remind me again of that beating up. It's over for me. *(Waves his hands in the air to show exasperation.)* Like the Aids thing. That's over too. Over completely. They found a cure.

MARK: *(Shakes his head.)* It's not over.

PAUL: It's over. Dead.

MARK: *(Softly.)* No.

PAUL: I'm tired of you talking about the bad things in the past. Why should we - why should I, who never really knew it, keep on being reminded of it?

MARK: You can't wipe it out. Aids happened. The bad times happened. Those bad times killed so many. *(Angrily.)* You're not stupid. You're not a robot. You know what pain is like. Can't you imagine their pain?

PAUL: No, and I don't want to. *(Pause.)* It's not my pain. *(Contemptuously.)* Those men who died.

MARK: It's not over for some even now.

PAUL: It's none of my business. It happened to them.

MARK: *(Now really angry.)* And who are them exactly?

PAUL: *(Shouting.)* The whole war crew. The veterans.

MARK: The dead as well as the living still cry out about it. They still ask why. *(Screams.)* Why? They scream out in my dreams.

PAUL: Then keep your dreams to yourself. *(Pause. Quietly.)* I'm late for work.

MARK: I employ you.

PAUL: I'm still late, and I like to get to work on time whether you employ me or not. Someone has to be practical around here. As it is I do nearly all the decision making.

MARK: *(Sarcastically.)* So, I've given way to your young creative enthusiasm.

PAUL: Shut up, Mark. I do a good job.

MARK: I'm not in love with a good job. Occasionally I would like to see the man underneath all that.

PAUL: I am all that you see. No more. No less. *(Pause.)* No layers. No hidden depths.

MARK: *(Slowly.)* I - I don't believe that.

PAUL: *(Goes to MARK and places both hands on MARK's shoulders. Looks at him.)* You'd better. I am only what you see. And must I keep on reminding you that I am not profound, that I am not meaningful, that I don't have a bloody soul - *(Pushes MARK away.)* - and that I like it that way? Simple surfaces, that's what I like. Unlike you I don't and can't suffer.

MARK: If I really believed that -

PAUL: *(Quietly.)* Yes? You'd do what?

MARK: Nothing.

PAUL: Leave me?

MARK: Don't put words into my mouth.

PAUL: And then isn't Alex coming back to add the depth that is missing in me? *(Pause.)* Isn't that part of the reason why you asked him back?

MARK: He has been away for twenty years. He disappeared out of my life.

PAUL: Well, there's lots of mysterious depths to that. I wouldn't call·that a surface job. *(Pause.)* Did he disappear because he didn't match up to your high expectations?

MARK: You're being vicious now.

PAUL: He didn't match up, so he went. I know I don't match up, but it doesn't make me consider going.

MARK: *(Slowly.)* I don't know why he did what he did.

PAUL: Walk out on you?

MARK: It wasn't as simple as that.

PAUL: Of course not. There were profound reasons. Must have been to do with all the black clothes you wore during those years. *(Pause.)* By the way, was that to do with all the funerals?

(Silence. MARK turns away from him.)

PAUL: Just a thought.

MARK: I didn't ask him to come back.

PAUL: What did he say to you that moved you to say he could come back?

MARK: He's been living in Paris for the past eighteen years. He's broke.

PAUL: So he wants a meal ticket?

MARK: He wants a chance to get back on his feet.

PAUL: Are you the only member of the old regime that will have him?

MARK: Yes. *(Coldly.)* Maybe I am just that. The only one who will have him.

PAUL: Shall I pack my bags now? The having has Biblical undertones, or overtones, or whatever it is they call it.

MARK: I'll help him back on his feet.

PAUL: *(Sneering.)* You poor sucker.

MARK: No doubt.

PAUL: Presumably he knows you are doing alright?

MARK: He knows I'm still in media.

PAUL: And what did he do in Paris all these years?

MARK: I don't know.

PAUL: Suppose he didn't have time to tell you on the phone.

MARK: That's right.

PAUL: Let's hope he didn't fail with a home for wounded animals. I'd hate him to give you lessons on that, you don't already know.

(Doorbell rings.)

PAUL: That's my lift. I'll see you later.

MARK: You haven't washed.

PAUL: I'll do it at the office.

MARK: Invite Frank in for a coffee.

PAUL: It's against our work rules. Remember?

MARK: Ring me from the studio. *(Pause.)* I'll be in late today.

PAUL: What's new?

(Doorbell rings again.)

MARK: You'd better go.

PAUL: Yes.

BLACKOUT

SCENE SIX

(MARK is alone on stage. He looks out at the audience from the front of the stage, then turns and goes to the back of the stage. He stands there without moving. ALEX enters, stage right. He is carrying a suitcase. He puts it down,

then exits. MARK turns round and looks at the suitcase. He raises his hands to his face and covers his eyes. ALEX re-enters with a second suitcase. He looks at MARK, then places the second suitcase beside the first. MARK doesn't take his hands away from his face but his mouth opens wide as if to scream. He remains silent. ALEX exits, then quickly re-enters with the third and last suitcase. MARK lowers his hands. His mouth closes. He looks at ALEX in silence. ALEX slowly moves towards him, and stops slightly to the right of him. He bends his head forward and kisses MARK on the mouth. MARK rushes forward, leaving ALEX standing at the back of the stage. He is gasping as if he cannot breathe and stops at the edge of the stage staring out at the audience. ALEX begins to move forward to join him. This scene is to be acted with the maximum ritual.)

MARK: One, Two, Three, Four, Five, Six - *(Then in a rush.)* - Seven, Eight, Nine, Ten, Eleven, Twelve, Thirteen, Fourteen, Fifteen, Sixteen, Seventeen, Eighteen, Nineteen - *(Gasps, crying out.)* - Twenty. *(Turns to face ALEX who is now directly behind him.)* Twenty years!

BLACKOUT

SCENE SEVEN

(MARK and ALEX. Stage brightly lit. Three suitcases to the right of stage. Scene opens with MARK and ALEX staring at each other.)

ALEX: So many questions.

MARK: Yes.

ALEX: *(Looks around.)* The place is alright.

MARK: *(Slight pause.)* You know I don't live here alone?

ALEX: Right. *(Wanders round the stage.)* When I rang
        you said you shared with someone. Paul - that his
        name?

MARK: Yes.

ALEX: He sounds a very correct man. Correct men
        always have names you can't shorten or lengthen.
        (Pause.) Young?

MARK: Mid-twenties.

ALEX: Young.

MARK: Look, I -

ALEX: Does he mind me coming to stay? I mean you
        did tell him it was only temporary, until I find a
        job, and get settled? He does know all that?

MARK: Yes.

ALEX: I don't want any misunderstanding. *(Pause.)* Are
        you in love with him?

MARK: Alex, can we take this a bit slower? You've just
        arrived and I feel I'm in an interrogation room.

ALEX: You always said I talked too much. I like to talk
        remember? Not changed in that direction. *(Looks
        round him. Stands still.)* You live in a neat part
        of London. You work near here?

MARK: Not far.

ALEX: You get together a lot of programmes? *(Pause.)*
        S'pose that's a silly question. What's a TV
        Channel for if it's not for lots of programmes? I
        don't watch TV much anymore. *(Pause.)* You
        almost got me involved the media business. Have
        you got Paul working for you as well?

MARK: He's better than I am.

ALEX: I don't believe that.

MARK: It's true. He knows the new scenes. *(Slight pause.)* I'm older, Alex, and out of touch. Or hadn't you noticed?

(Silence.)

ALEX: *(Uncomfortable.)* It's nice here.

MARK: Your room is at the top of the house. It's a bit of a mess.

ALEX: Never minded a mess.

MARK: I'll let you sort out the space you want. *(Pause.)* There are lots of cupboards.

(Awkward silence.)

ALEX: Well -

MARK: Well -

ALEX: I thought this was going to be different. *(Pause.)* You haven't said how I look.

MARK: You look alright.

ALEX: Said with real conviction.

MARK: I mean it.

ALEX: Do you? *(Long pause.)* Well, my hair has thinned, and I'm a bit lined around the face. Still got all my teeth.

MARK: You sound as if you are selling yourself for a job. I'm not interested in the details of how you have physically changed, Alex.

ALEX: *(Comes up to MARK.)* You look well.

MARK: *(Moves away.)* I am well.

ALEX: I didn't mean -

MARK: Well, that was a long time ago. The damage caused to my system left its traces, but basically I am very well indeed.

ALEX: I'm glad. *(Pause.)* Look, I'm feeling uncomfortable around this. If we are going to talk about what happened, I would rather we did it now and got it out of the way.

MARK: I'm not sure we can ever get it out of the way, Alex.

ALEX: Bad way of putting it. Sorry. *(Pause.)* I paid for what I did. After all, you are the successful one now, aren't you? And well, just look at me - not much above a tramp at the moment. I haven't been for quite some time.

MARK: You want us to talk about you leaving me?

ALEX: I don't want to, but we will, so what I'm saying is let's get on with it.

MARK: You've just arrived.

ALEX: And if I am to stay as your guest I want a good atmosphere.

MARK: Are you asking me if I blame you?

ALEX: *(Quietly.)* Yes.

MARK: I blamed you. Very definitely at the time. *(Pause.)* It's a long way back now. I can't be sure how I feel.

ALEX: On the phone I almost had the feeling you wanted me back.

MARK: I loved you. I still would like to help.

ALEX: I loved you as well. But I had to go then. I couldn't cope with it.

MARK: Look, have a bath. See your room. We'll talk later. This isn't the appropriate time.

ALEX: No, please, I want you to understand that I had to disappear. I was running away from the whole thing. It wasn't you. It wasn't. *(Pause.)* The Aids issue was too much for me to cope with.

MARK: I know all that. But it just wasn't an issue, it was a person you were leaving.

ALEX: I realised that - later.

MARK: But you didn't return later. *(Turns his back on ALEX.)* As we are talking about this - perhaps really for the first time - can I ask you how?

ALEX: How what?

MARK: *(After a long pause.)* How could you walk out on me when you knew I thought I was going to die?

(Long silence.)

ALEX: I was afraid.

MARK: You weren't personally threatened by your own death.

ALEX: I was threatened by yours. I just wasn't up to it. I know when we met I said I'd stand by if it happened -as you said you'd stand by me if I caught the virus, but - *(Pause.)* - we don't always keep our promises in life do we?

MARK: *(Angrily.)* Don't say we. It was you.

ALEX: Me. *(Slight pause.)* I'm not good at keeping my word.

MARK: So why did you go?

ALEX: I've just said -

MARK: The truth. All of it.

ALEX: I've said -

MARK: Not all of it.

ALEX: I don't know what else I can say.

MARK: What weren't you capable of exactly?

(Silence.)

ALEX: Seeing you die.

(They look at each other for a while. ALEX looks away first.)

MARK: A lot felt fear of a lover dying. Coping with it. The pain of it. A lot beside you ran away. I know all that, and I understand it. And you know I know all that.

ALEX: It's years ago. *(Pause.)* I've remembered enough. Why should I remember more? *(Shouts.)* Why should I remember more?

MARK: Because you are here. You are here, and I am not dead. I am alive. You owe it to me to tell me everything.

ALEX: I heard in Paris years ago that you had survived. Just after the celebrations. All those balloons and fucking parties.

MARK: But you never contacted.

ALEX: You weren't dead, but it was.

MARK: You mean between us?

ALEX: Yes.

MARK: I see.

(Silence.)

MARK: *(Slowly.)* I thought I was going to die. I was terrified. I wanted you near me. And you walked out on me, leaving no address, no way of finding you.

ALEX: I had to.

MARK: *(Shouts.)* Why?

ALEX: If you hadn't wanted me to stay, I would have stayed. I couldn't stand your begging. I couldn't stand the suffocating way you wanted to bind me into caring. You suffocated me by needing me. *(Paces room.)* Oh, the sickness scared me. The possibility, however remote it was of getting infected, scared too - but beyond all that, you - you scared me. The hunger in you to cling on, to eat me, so there was nothing left of me. That would have killed me.

MARK: You were a coward.

ALEX: Yes.

MARK: And how does it feel now to see me standing here, twenty years on, alive?

ALEX: I don't want to -

MARK: *(Screams.)* How does it feel?

ALEX: You really want to know?

MARK: Yes.

ALEX: *(Hitting MARK physically with his hands.)* I hate you still for making me feel guilty. I hated you then, and now looking at you, I know why I hated you, and why I still feel it. You wanted to eat out my life, suck it out. You wanted to kill me too.

MARK: *(Shouting.)* That's not true.

ALEX: True. *(Stops hitting at MARK.)* Those of us who were expected to stand by and watch all of you

die, do you know what we went through? We
were survivors as well. We survived you. Do you
know how we blamed and suffered, how we
hated you - all of you for hating us? *(Violently.)*
For years I thought you had died. I expected you
to die.

*(ALEX stands back. Looks at MARK, then he lunges
forward and hits MARK so hard that MARK falls to the
ground.)*

ALEX: That is for not dying. For making me care.

(ALEX falls back exhausted.)

MARK: *(Struggles to his feet.)* Get out.

ALEX: Yes.

(Long silence. Neither move.)

ALEX: I'll take the blame. I did then. *(Pause.)* Nothing
          has changed.

(Silence.)

MARK: *(Quietly.)* Stay.

ALEX: *(Laughing.)* Nothing has changed.

MARK: Yes, it has. You said you cared.

ALEX: Why should those few words mean more than all
          the rest?

MARK: Because you said them with passion. There was
          nothing planned in what you did or said just then.

ALEX: I haven't changed. I'm out for me.

MARK: I know.

ALEX: And I'd betray you again. Don't think for one
          moment that I wouldn't be capable of it.

MARK: *(Slowly.)* What happened in Paris?

ALEX: I behaved in the same way as I behaved here.

MARK: Can you talk about it?

ALEX: I wasn't ever much good at finding jobs. You know that. Easy living was my motto, before I met you, while I was with you, and afterwards. *(Pause.)* Then in Paris I met this actor. Experimental theatre. He had his own company. He taught me about performance art and soon I realised that I was interested. I had an instinct for it. I learnt quickly and I helped him run his company. I also became his lover.

MARK: Did you love him?

ALEX: As much as I loved you.

MARK: What happened?

ALEX: A visit to the clinic happened. He said he never wanted to be tested, but then I gave him syphilis, and while he was there at the clinic with me, he had the test. *(Pause.)* It was positive. I then had the test and I was negative. The cure was round the corner, but it came too late for him. Unlike you he was already very ill when he tested, and soon he was dying.

MARK: And you left him?

ALEX: I left him. *(Pause.)* He committed suicide in an hotel room.

(MARK stares at him in silence.)

ALEX: I hated myself. Again. I couldn't work. I went to pieces. I became - what's the point of describing what I became? I hustled, and I hated. *(Pause.)* For years. Then time caught up with me, and I looked in the mirror and knew that if the selfish me was to survive, then I'd have to save myself.

MARK: So it was then you decided to ring me?

ALEX: *(Laughs.)* No. No, you were the last resort. *(Pause.)* I met a twenty year old boy, and went and lived with him. He cooked my meals, mended my clothes, and in return I said I love you, and fucked him regularly.

MARK: Did you love him?

ALEX: As much as I loved you and the dancer. I can love easily. You should know that.

MARK: And you left him?

ALEX: He left me. He found someone younger and prettier, and then I remembered you.

MARK: *(Coldly.)* I think you should take your luggage upstairs now.

ALEX: You sure you want me here?

MARK: For as long as you need to be.

ALEX: *(Slowly.)* Can I ask you one question?

MARK: Yes.

ALEX: What did you see in me?

MARK: What I wanted to see in you I suppose.

ALEX: That's not love either.

(PAUL enters. ALEX is about to pick up a suitcase. He stops, looks at PAUL and smiles.)

PAUL: I didn't expect you to arrive so soon.

ALEX: I'm sorry.

PAUL: Don't apologise to me. I didn't invite you.

ALEX: I invited myself, or didn't Mark tell you?

PAUL: It takes two -

ALEX: Oh yes, of course.

MARK: Paul, Alex is a guest here. You may not like that, but I want you to treat him -

ALEX: *(Interrupting.)* How should he treat me Mark? With respect?

PAUL: You're well dressed for someone who is pleading poverty.

ALEX: *(Laughs.)* I think I'm going to like you.

PAUL: *(Ignoring him.)* Mark, I need a loan. I've got an unexpected dinner tonight.

ALEX: Don't you pay him well Mark?

PAUL: A temporary stranglehold at the bank. *(To ALEX.)* How do you get on with your bank?

MARK: How much do you need?

ALEX: Dinner money comes expensive.

PAUL: In Paris maybe. Here, some of us eat more cheaply.

MARK: Take my card. It's in my coat.

PAUL: See you later. *(Exits.)*

ALEX: *(Stares after him.)* I like him. He's not soft is he? In fact he's probably tougher than I ever was.

MARK: Before you meet him again, I must ask you to be careful.

ALEX: What about?

MARK: Never to tell him I had Aids.

ALEX: *(Smiles.)* A house rule?

MARK: I'd lose him if he knew.

ALEX: I thought those days were over. What has he got to run from?

MARK: He is ashamed of the history of Aids, like quite a few of his generation. They wear bright clothes, and lead bright lives, or hadn't you noticed?

ALEX: They always wear bright clothes in Paris.

MARK: Didn't you meet people like him there?

ALEX: I suppose so.

MARK: So be careful. He's been beaten up recently and part of the taunting was about what we went through. He hates Aids, and even if I don't respect that I have to try and understand it. *(Pause.)* Its all very healthy out there now.

ALEX: Tell me exactly where my room is.

BLACKOUT

SCENE EIGHT
(Soft lighting. PAUL alone on stage. He is lying on the floor surrounded by weights. He is doing exercises. ALEX enters quietly, and stands for a while watching him. PAUL stands up and continues exercising, ignoring ALEX. He is sweaty and then suddenly he becomes out of breath. He puts down the weights. ALEX coughs, and PAUL is forced to look at him. He looks at him, then turns away.)

PAUL: I don't like being watched.

ALEX: I used to do that at your age.

PAUL: I'm not particularly interested.

ALEX: You work hard.

PAUL: Well, the whole thing isn't exactly for decoration, is it? *(Picks up a weight, exercises, then puts it down. Turns to ALEX.)* By the way, how long are you staying?

ALEX: Are you paying for my meals?

PAUL: No.

ALEX: Then I don't think it is really any of your business.

PAUL: We take up the same air space. That is my business.

ALEX: Can I try the weights?

PAUL: Aren't you a bit out of practice?

ALEX: Do I look out of practice?

PAUL: I'd have to touch your body to find out.

ALEX: Feel free.

PAUL: I am free. No, thank you.

(ALEX goes to PAUL and pulls him to him hard. PAUL struggles and pushes him away.)

PAUL: Don't try that one again.

ALEX: I was only testing.

PAUL: Testing what?

ALEX: Tell you sometime.

PAUL: Piss off.

ALEX: Aren't you curious about me at all? It's been four weeks now, and you haven't asked me anything.

PAUL: *(Smiling.)* Have they got any new architectural plans for Paris?

(Silence.)

PAUL: When are you going back?

ALEX: When I'm ready.

PAUL: So you are going back?

ALEX: Sometime.

PAUL: *(His defences breaking down a little.)* What's it
          like there?

ALEX: You'd like Paris.

PAUL: Would I?

ALEX: If you're anything like me you would.

PAUL: Who says I'm anything like you?

ALEX: Simon. Mark. I can see it as well. *(Pause.)*
          Mirror, mirror on the wall -

PAUL: Me. I'm younger. And I'm better looking.

(Both unexpectedly laugh.)

ALEX: Well, that's broken the ice.

PAUL: Pretty confident about your charms, aren't you?

ALEX: Aren't you?

PAUL: I can see what Mark saw in you.

*(Long pause. They look at each other. Almost as if they are
about to embrace.)*

ALEX: Do you find me attractive?

(PAUL turns away. Lifts a weight.)

ALEX: I asked –

PAUL: I know what you asked.

ALEX: You'll wear yourself out.

PAUL: I know what I'm doing. *(Pause. Lowers weight.
          Turns to ALEX.)* Why did you leave Mark?

ALEX: It's a long story.

PAUL: *(Takes off his T shirt and towels the sweat off his
          body.)* Did you find the possessive streak hard to
          take?

ALEX: I could have coped with that - on its own.

PAUL: Don't tell me there was something more interesting. *(Pause.)* I've got it. Simon. He's always been secretly in love with Simon. Did you know that poor bastard is still around? He's been a chemist all these years, and oh God does he think he does good! *(Pause.)* And another thing. Why hasn't he been around since you've been here? Rumour has it he's in the house today, but hiding from you.

ALEX: Doesn't like me.

PAUL: Was he jealous of you?

ALEX: It's all in the past.

PAUL: I like the past when it's to do with my future.

ALEX: Do you intend to stay with Mark?

PAUL: *(Laughs.)* That's a neat move. Are you going to persuade me to go so you can step in?

ALEX: He's no longer interested in me. I'm sure even you have noticed that there is hardly an erotic charge between us. *(Pause.)* He loves you.

PAUL: Sure. I'm cute.

ALEX: That's right.

(ALEX goes to PAUL and holds him again. Kisses him on the mouth. With one hand he plays with PAUL's nipples, with the other he caresses PAUL's sex. PAUL doesn't push him away. They hold each other for a while, then separate.)

ALEX: Turn you on?

PAUL: *(Avoiding this.)* What's the full story behind you coming here?

(ALEX picks up a weight and clearly shows off to PAUL that he can do it as well, if not better than him.)

PAUL: I'm impressed.

ALEX: *(Puts down weight.)* I'm not washed up, despite what you might have heard about me.

PAUL: I asked you, what's the full story?

ALEX: *(Coldly.)* I left Mark twenty years ago. He told you that, didn't he?

PAUL: Yes.

ALEX: I left for a number of reasons. One, I was no longer in love with him, if I ever was, and two, I wasn't going to go under with him. *(Long pause.)* I've been told not to tell you the real reason. It seems there is something you hate more than anything else.

PAUL: *(Goes to ALEX. Faces him.)* Tell me.

ALEX: Mark had Aids.

(Long silence. PAUL laughs, steps back. PAUL looks shocked, but says nothing. PAUL bends down and picks up a weight, raises it above his head, then lowers it slowly. PAUL sits down on the floor. ALEX sits beside him, putting his arm around PAUL. PAUL neither rejects him nor encourages him.)

ALEX: Mark had Aids.

PAUL: I heard you the first time.

ALEX: I was in the clear. I was never infected by the virus.

PAUL: *(Stares at ALEX.)* Is that why you walked out on him?

ALEX: If I had been in love with him, stayed in love with him, then maybe I would have stayed. He wanted me entirely there, and I couldn't be. I just didn't feel enough. *(Pause.)* Simon was there. He was better for him than me.

PAUL: So then you went to Paris?

ALEX: Modelling jobs paid well. I was given plenty of jobs in Paris. At one time I was a very successful model. *(Pause.)* It was the kind of life I wanted. Looking at you I find it hard to believe you are not bored in this atmosphere. Mark is so -what's the word for it - stark? He's all black and white, all shadow and depth. Like an old movie.

PAUL: Yeah....and I'm cinemascope and bright colour.

ALEX: I was. *(Hugs PAUL to him.)* Little brother. We are alike. You remind me so much of how I was. I've watched you. I've waited.

PAUL: *(Quietly.)* For what?

ALEX: For you to take me seriously.

PAUL: *(Stands. Looks down at ALEX.)* Are you telling me the truth about Mark?

ALEX: *(Nods his head.)* The truth.

PAUL: *(Slowly.)* I don't feel anything. I thought I'd feel disgust or anger - but then why should I? Aids happened, and I believed him when he said he wasn't infected by it. *(Pause.)* Oh, I know people he knew died, but his own body infected? I never thought of it happening to him. *(Long pause.)* I see old photos of it sometimes. The emaciated bodies. That emptied out look, as if their whole personalities had been scooped out. I look at the photos, and I just wish it had never happened. It's a nightmare, even now, but it's not my nightmare. I suppose I'm callous, but I can't feel any sorrow about those years. *(Pause.)* In the last century, after the Second World War, young people wanted to forget. I've never read anywhere that they were blamed for it.

ALEX: *(Stands beside him.)* You'll leave him now won't you?

PAUL: *(Smiles.)* Is that what you want?

ALEX: I shall go back to Paris. I'm not quite as poor as Mark may have said. I told him that because I got into a bit of trouble there, and I needed to get back here for a while.

PAUL: Real trouble?

ALEX: I did a bit of drugs. The Police got interested. *(Pause.)* It'll blow over. There's someone else there who will take the blame. As soon as I hear he has, I'll be free to return.

PAUL: Sounds exciting.

ALEX: I've made better livings, but I've got enough - just not at the moment.

PAUL: *(Quickly. A note of panic in his voice.)* There's someone behind the door.

ALEX: Mark has probably been listening.

PAUL: I want time to think. I don't want him to be told I know before I've thought things through. *(Listens.)* It's him. I know he's there.

(SIMON enters. He looks at both of them in silence. Then he moves slowly towards them.)

SIMON: You look right together.

PAUL: I'm ignoring that, Simon.

SIMON: You won't ignore it for long. I've only got to take one look at you both to know that there's interest there.

ALEX: How clever of you Simon.

PAUL: Alex and I were talking.

SIMON: Oh yes, talking. Fine thing isn't it, talking? How lucky we are that it differentiates us from the animals. *(Goes to ALEX and mockingly caresses his face.)* What animal have you become, Alex?

ALEX: Trying to provoke me?

SIMON: I've waited twenty years for it Alex. Don't spoil my pleasure.

PAUL: I'll wait in another room until you boys have finished. *(Moves towards exit.)*

ALEX: Don't go.

SIMON: *(To PAUL.)* Well, you can't deny your new friend that request can you?

PAUL: *(Sits down again on the floor.)* Be brief, Simon. It's boring.

SIMON: How cute you look down there Paul. Harmless as a pet animal. *(Turns to ALEX.)* Not like you.

(Silence.)

SIMON: I remember twenty years ago, another pet animal, but he didn't look like you, Paul. He had no malice in him. He was cute too, but not in your way. He was totally, totally harmless. *(Pause. Looks at ALEX.)* But, he had a master.

ALEX: You are talking rubbish, Simon.

SIMON: He had a master who got tired of him. *(Pause.)* Who got tired of him being a sick pet. A sick, unloved pet. And do you know what this master wanted to do, Paul?

PAUL: If this is Winnie the Pooh territory, Simon, then shove off. You're not only being boring, you're being boringly obscure.

SIMON: It's a pity you didn't read Winnie the Pooh stories, Paul. They might have taught you some basic humanity.

ALEX: Leave us alone, Simon.

SIMON: *(Mockingly.)* Oh, the master giving orders again. Making decisions.

PAUL: I said to shove off, Simon.

SIMON: *(Almost gently.)* Alright Paul, but first I want to tell you something about this man.

PAUL: *(Looking up at Simon.)* Is this more according to the Gospel of St Mark?

SIMON: Twenty years ago, Alex came to me, and he was crying almost sincerely. He said he was scared about Mark, and that he couldn't bear to see him suffer. He had heard of a remedy for Mark you see, and he wanted my approval, and my gifts of persuasion to work upon Mark to convince him of the remedy.

ALEX: It's all lies, Paul.

SIMON: He was scared because Mark was developing the full-blown syndrome. He was sorry of course, and oh, so helpless, and after weeks and weeks of worry, he had found a way out that he thought was best suited for Mark. *(Pause.)* I'm trying to remember his exact words.

ALEX: Stop it, Simon.

SIMON: Can't you see he's afraid, Paul? He knows I'm not lying.

ALEX: Paul, he's trying to destroy again –

191

SIMON: *(Wheels round on ALEX angrily.)* And who here is the real expert on human destruction? Didn't you ask me to persuade Mark to go to Holland? To go to Holland to be put down - like an animal?

(Long silence. The three of them do not move. Simon breaks the silence by bending down and speaking to Paul.)

SIMON: It's true what I have told you.

PAUL: *(Coldly.)* So?

SIMON: *(Draws back slowly, then stands up.)* Is that all you can say? So?

PAUL: Would it have been such a bad thing, euthanasia, if he had developed Aids? *(Pause.)* It's clean and quick.

SIMON: *(Quietly.)* Speech really does differentiate us from the animals.

PAUL: Poor boring Simon.

SIMON: *(Turns to Alex.)* And what do you have to say?

PAUL: Don't feel you have to answer him.

ALEX: He's right, Paul. I did go to him. I did think it would be for the best, when he really got sick. There were ways in Holland to put an end to it humanely.

SIMON: *(Shouts.)* Mark was your lover, you bastard, not your dog.

PAUL: *(To Alex.)* Simon has always been over emotional. If I had been in your position I would have done exactly the same thing.

SIMON: No one asked Mark.

PAUL: I thought Alex came to you precisely for that - to ask Mark?

SIMON: I'm going to leave you to each other now. I don't want to be in the same room with either of you any more. I've hit an area of darkness here that is worse than anything Mark or I went through.

PAUL: Were you sick too, Simon?

SIMON: I was not sick. I had Aids, but I wasn't sick. And I had the strength to carry Mark over to a safer side.

PAUL: You were in love with him.

SIMON: *(Slowly.)* I was his friend.

BLACKOUT

SCENE NINE

(Bright lights. SIMON seated. PAUL enters, and stands behind him. PAUL laughs and moves forward facing SIMON. SIMON ignores him. PAUL walks around him, looking at him contemptuously. SIMON puts his hand in his pocket and takes out a tube of vitamin pills. SIMON remains still while PAUL walks round him a second time.)

PAUL: The dog waiting for his master's return? *(Laughs. Bends down and peers into SIMON's face.)* Yap, yap, yap.

(SIMON stands up and PAUL sits on the floor.)

PAUL: Doggie brought his best friend a present?

(SIMON turns his back on him.)

PAUL: What a present! Strong vitamin pills to keep the master's pecker up? *(Pause.)* S'pose you took a lot of those when you were ill. What a good doggie chemist. *(Turns his head at the sound of a noise.)* Master coming home now.

(MARK enters with ALEX. ALEX has visibly had too much to drink. He ruffles PAUL's hair, and PAUL moves away from him and gets up. SIMON looks at MARK and hands him the pills in silence.)

MARK: *(Smiles.)* Thank you.

PAUL: He's ignoring me, Mark. Here I was, trying to be the perfect host and I can't even get a smile out of him.

MARK: Go to bed Paul.

PAUL: *(Mockingly salutes.)* Yes, Sir.

(PAUL exits.)

MARK: *(To SIMON.)* You shouldn't have waited. The pills could have waited.

ALEX: *(To SIMON.)* Did you think I'd steal them, Simon, if I saw them first? *(Takes pills from MARK and looks at them.)* Not my sort. *(Rubs at his sex.)* My energy levels don't need propping up.

MARK: *(Slowly.)* I'm tired.

ALEX: Come on, let's have a drink together. I need another drink. Five is not nearly enough for a celebration.

SIMON: *(Looks at ALEX.)* What are you celebrating, Alex?

ALEX: Well, that made him talk. *(Pause.)* My return home, of course.

SIMON: I see.

ALEX: No, you don't. I call anywhere I stay more than a night a home. Don't look worried, Simon, I've no intention of outstaying my welcome. *(To Mark.)* Drink, Mark?

MARK: I must go to bed.

ALEX: Just one last one, to take with your old buddy's
          vitamins.

MARK: *(To SIMON. Gently.)* I really am all in. Can you
          see yourself out?

ALEX: *(Looks at SIMON.)* Leaving him alone with me?

(SIMON moves to exit.)

ALEX: Oh, come on Simon, you can stay for a drink.
          Tell him to stay for a drink, Mark. I'm too drunk
          to hate him.

MARK: *(To SIMON.)* See yourself out.

(MARK exits.)

ALEX: Well, well, well, all alone after all these years.
          Didn't expect that after our last encounter.

SIMON: *(Quietly.)* Why don't you just leave him alone?
          (Grabs at Alex's arm.) Why?

ALEX: *(Pushes SIMON away.)* Drink?

SIMON: Fuck the drink.

ALEX: Never used to say that. I remember you with a
          bottle in one hand and poppers up your nose with
          the other. *(Pause.)* Come to think of it, you didn't
          look as if you were having fun then. Such a
          handsome, serious face you had. *(Comes up and
          peers at SIMON closely.)* Still handsome, in a
          leftover sort of way. *(Exits to get drink. Talks off
          stage.)* I'm pouring you one anyway.

SIMON: I don't want it.

ALEX: Can't hear. *(Enters with two drinks.)* Vodka. You
          used to like vodka. Do you remember that night
          we all went out together and you met this boy
          and got him so drunk on vodka that he asked you

to marry him? He was nice if I remember. Wouldn't have minded marrying him myself. *(Pause.)* Pity you didn't though. It would have had you settled by now, instead of roaming round other peoples' houses. Snooping at doors. *(He tries to hand SIMON a drink.)*

SIMON: *(Pushes his hand away.)* I don't want it.

ALEX: Two for me. *(Puts one down. Drinks slowly from the other.)*

SIMON: Can't you see you will destroy Mark if you remain? If you take Paul away from him? *(Pause.)* That is what you intend to do, isn't it?

ALEX: He's got you. Who else would come round late at night looking ridiculous with vitamin pills?

SIMON: *(Angrily grabs at ALEX and pushes him against a wall.)* Do you know what I want to do to you? I want to smash your head in against the wall. I want to see your blood. I want to prove you have got blood. *(ALEX is scared and tries to break free. SIMON is stronger.)* I want to see your blood running down the wall. I'd like to strip you naked and see the blood running down you. *(Pause. Quietly.)* I could do it. I could gag you with one hand and do it with the other. Paul gets to sleep quickly. He wouldn't hear you cry. Mark would hear you cry, and think it's just another nightmare.

ALEX: Let me go.

SIMON: Simon says no.

ALEX: I'll scream out.

SIMON: I'll cover your mouth at the first sound of a cry.

ALEX: Let me go.

SIMON: I've had fantasies about torturing you. Would you like to hear about some of them? *(Covers ALEX's mouth.)* Now you won't scream. I heard you scream once years ago when you cut your finger on a razor blade. Mark sucked your blood to make it better. How he loved you. *(Pushes his hand harder against ALEX's mouth.)* How he loved you and trusted you, and I stood by and watched. *(Pause.)* I wanted to kill you then. I saw that razor blade and I imagined slitting your cute little throat with it. *(Pause.)* I could do it now. I could satisfy the dreams I've had of punishing you.

(ALEX is very frightened. He struggles and SIMON tightens his grip on him, still covering ALEX's mouth with his other hand. He pushes him forward. He is behind ALEX.)

SIMON: Now I'm going to take my hand away, and if you so much as begin to scream I'll hit you so hard you'll wear a bruise as a badge over your face for months.

(SIMON takes away his hand. ALEX is now literally too scared to cry out. SIMON pulls at ALEX's clothes, pulling down his trousers. Then he pushes his own trousers down to his knees. ALEX is shaking with fear, then screams as he is pushed further forward. SIMON penetrates him, thrusting into him savagely. He begins to groan and despite himself ALEX groans as well, but mixed in with the groans are small whimperings and cries. At last the thrusting stops and after mockingly kissing ALEX on the neck SIMON pushes him away from him. SIMON stands up, adjusting his clothes, and ALEX crawls away from him still whimpering and painfully adjusting his own clothes as well.)

SIMON: Get up.

(ALEX crawls into a corner, then crawls out again, as if realising there is no place left that is safe.)

SIMON: Or crawl. I've wanted to see you crawl.

ALEX: *(Whimpering.)* Leave me alone.

SIMON: You like to be left alone, don't you? You wreck things and people, then you go into hiding and you plan your next moves.

ALEX: *(Remains on the floor, leaning against a wall.)* Give me my drink. Please.

SIMON: Crawl for that too.

ALEX: Please. I need it.

SIMON: Scare you, did I?

ALEX: Just give me the bloody drink.

SIMON: *(Hands it to him.)* Did I sober you up?

ALEX: *(Drinks quickly. Looks at SIMON.)* You can't hurt me.

SIMON: I know that. I could tear your flesh apart, but I'd only hurt the skin. There's nothing inside you to hurt.

(Silence.)

ALEX: *(Quietly.)* I feel.

SIMON: Not pain you don't.

ALEX: *(Slowly.)* You don't know me.

SIMON: You have sobered up. That's sober talk, Alex.

ALEX: I'm going to leave Mark. Don't worry about that. He's all yours. *(Pause.)* I don't know why I came back really. Part of me wanted to see him again. Part of me even wanted to see you again.

SIMON: You'll have me crying.

ALEX: In Paris, I never believed they'd find a cure. I thought you'd both die. I imagined you in hospital together, sort of finding each other, as it were, at the last minute. *(Pause.)* I hoped you would. But then someone you both knew told me you'd survived. And I got drunk that night too. I didn't want you both alive. It would have been so much neater the other way, and I'd never have felt this - this feeling of unfinished business here.

SIMON: But it is finished.

ALEX: Yes.

SIMON: You've seen us.

ALEX: Yes.

SIMON: Why Paul though? *(ALEX gets to his feet.)* Why Paul?

ALEX: He's there.

SIMON: Is that all?

ALEX: He's company. We could share things. *(Pause.)* I've been alone you see. I want the company of someone like me.

(Silence.)

SIMON: Can you imagine something for a moment? I want you to imagine what it's like to die. A while ago, for a moment, you believed I could kill you. I felt it in your body. And you were afraid. *(Pause.)* Imagine what it's like to die.

ALEX: *(The panic returns.)* Stop it. You've had your fun.

SIMON: Imagine gasping for breath, and everything going dark. Like sinking into water. It's heavy and its dark, and underneath the darkness there are terrible sounds. The sounds of death are terrible.

ALEX: *(Shouts.)* Stop.

SIMON: I've been there, and so has Mark. We've heard the door slam against our bodies. Underneath the surface of death we've hammered our way back. It's terrible that hammering. It's the worst sound there is. *(Shakes ALEX.)* And I want you to hear it. I want you to imagine it. Feel the screams and the fighting, Alex. Feel it. *(Shakes ALEX violently, pushing him down on to the floor. The violence gets out of control. SIMON cannot stop hitting ALEX or banging him against the floor. As SIMON is assaulting ALEX he shouts the following words at him.)* Death, Alex. It'll happen. One day it will happen and you will have nowhere to run, and no one to help you. You'll fall into that darkness and you'll have no one to help you.

ALEX: *(Screams out.)* I'll take Paul with me.

SIMON: Into death?

ALEX: Away from here.

SIMON: It won't help you. The last day will come for you, and there will be no love, no pity. You won't even have me frightening you. You won't have the consolation of knowing you are going under while someone else is watching. *(Pause.)* You have solitude branded on you for life, Alex.

ALEX: *(Staggers to his feet and reaches out for the glass. Drinks.)* I'm leaving.

SIMON: Run.

ALEX: *(Pause. Screams.)* You're proud I suppose you've made me run?

SIMON: *(Shakes his head slowly. Wearily.)* I can't hate you enough to feel proud. I just want it to be quiet for Mark. I want you to leave him alone.

ALEX: *(Goes up to SIMON.)* Twenty years ago I felt something for you. Now I know what it was. It was fear. *(Pause.)* Tell me -

SIMON: What?

ALEX: Never mind.

SIMON: What can I tell you?

ALEX: Tell me he didn't suffer too much because of me.

SIMON: *(Laughs.)* You idiot. You can't weigh it in the scales. I don't know what you did to him. I can't be your judge. But you can judge yourself. That's all you have.

ALEX: *(Backs away.)* Shut up.

SIMON: *(Softly.)* That's all you have.

BLACKOUT

SCENE TEN

(Stage in darkness. Slowly lightens. Bright lights. PAUL is packing a suitcase. He has a pile of clothes in front of him. Slowly, methodically, he puts them into the case. MARK is seated, watching him in silence. A look of total despair on MARK's face. PAUL picks up a tie and holds it up.)

PAUL: This is yours. *(Silence. He places it beside the case. Continues packing. Then he holds up a shirt.)* Yours as well.

MARK: I never saw him do this.

PAUL: *(Bored voice.)* Who?

MARK: Alex.

PAUL: Oh.

MARK: He -

(MARK stops talking. PAUL looks at him at last and smiles.)

PAUL: Alex disappeared without a trace. I know. Unlike Alex, because I am not like Alex, and I have got pretty tired of being compared to him by both you and Simon, I leave places quite openly and freely.

MARK: You call this freedom?

PAUL: I want to pack, I want to go quickly, and I want you - well, not to talk to me. *(Smiles again.)* Let's just leave things the way they are and say goodbye.

MARK: And I suppose you'll be ready to say that soon? In an hour? Less than an hour?

PAUL: The train goes in two hours.

MARK: You know he'll walk out on you as well? Paris won't be the romantic place he has perhaps described it as being.

PAUL: I'm not looking for romance. *(Closes the suitcase.)* That's finished.

MARK: What are you looking for?

PAUL: *(Slowly.)* I don't want to talk.

MARK: What are you looking for?

PAUL: A good time.

MARK: *(Laughs.)* With him?

PAUL: Without him if necessary. There are other attractions to Paris besides Alex.

MARK: You are - *(Stops.)*

PAUL: You have an irritating way of not finishing
         sentences. This one is probably an accusation. I
         am what precisely? An opportunist? Hardly. He's
         poor. I know that. He probably always will be.
         (Pause.) But Mark dear, I am not after money.

MARK: What then?

PAUL: You don't think it might be love?

MARK: It's not your speciality. Love.

PAUL: No, it's not.

MARK: Well then?

PAUL: He gives me a sense of freedom. *(Looks at
         MARK steadily.)* He's free of a past that you had
         and that I hate. He freed himself from Aids and
         he freed himself from you.

(Silence. MARK cries out quickly as if he had been hit.)

PAUL: Don't cry. It won't move me Mark. He freed
         himself from that kind of blackmail as well. He
         got away from the fear and the clinging.

MARK: *(Cries out.)* I did not cling. He told you that lie as
         well.

PAUL: You were a leech.

MARK: No.

PAUL: An emotional leech.

MARK: It's not true.

PAUL: He would have become sick too if you had had
         your way. But he wasn't going to let you.
         (Pause.) He was scared of sleeping with you
         because one day you threatened to sexually
         assault him. He was scared because you were
         looking for that one vulnerable time when he
         would have been receptive to infection.

MARK: *(Shouts.)* Do you really believe I could have behaved like that?

PAUL: He freed himself from the risk.

(Silence.)

MARK: Why do you hate us so much, Paul?

(PAUL shrugs his shoulders.)

MARK: All of us who are survivors?

PAUL: It's not really hate. It's like you still trail after you that contamination. As though you are proud that you were sick and that society was afraid of you.

MARK: *(Slowly.)* We were afraid of them. Do you know how they tortured us in so many ways? The useless drugs that they knew were useless? The humiliations of asking, of crawling for help when they cut back on helping people to die at home? *(Pause.)* So many died alone because the hospitals were full. *(Begins to circle round PAUL.)* I saw the inside of hospitals. Oh, so well. Let me tell you one story. Remember this if you remember nothing else once you've got to Paris. *(Long pause.)* A guy not much older than you, in a ward with four other people. An enclosed small ward. He was in a corner of that room, with a collapsed lung. He was in terrible pain, and across the space in an opposite bed was a man less ill than him. I should add before continuing that my friend was blind. Because of the chaos in those days and the lack of staff the rules in those rooms were not very clear. The man opposite him wanted to smoke, and he didn't give a damn about my friend's lung. He lit up, and the visitor he had with him lit up a cigarette as well, and when my friend asked them to stop he was subjected to verbal abuse. 'What right have you to stop us smoking?'- the man in the bed asked? And my friend tried to explain that it hurt him to breathe, that the smoke was bad for him. And do you know what the visitor shouted at him? He shouted: 'I'm not going to let a blind git like you tell us what to do'. My friend did nothing because he was blind and he was afraid of being hit. The violence of the streets was there on that ward. *(MARK stops circling. Looks at PAUL who won't look at him.)* Even in the wards we tortured each other. Men to men. No care. No love. The sound of the future sounded then. We began then to put the jackboots on of this future you love so much.

PAUL: In Paris at least I won't have to listen to this.

MARK: Freedom city. Don't you think they have survivors there?

PAUL: I won't be living with one. *(Pause.)* I'll choose the future, not the past.

MARK: You'll leave him too, won't you?

PAUL: Who knows?

MARK: Pastures green after a month. A healthy man who has always been healthy will come along, and there it will be, total liberty. 'cos Alex is not entirely free of the taint of Aids, is he? I mean he did know me, make love to me, was associated with the whole thing. Total freedom will mean getting rid of him as well.

(Silence. PAUL paces the room.)

MARK: I wonder that you don't walk out of the room now. You don't have to listen to me.

PAUL: You're right. I don't have to listen.

MARK: But you are listening.

PAUL: I'll leave.

(PAUL goes towards the exit. He stops, unable to leave.)

MARK: I didn't believe you could go.

PAUL: I will go.

MARK: You know I have something to say. Something
        you want to hear. You won't admit it but you are
        curious about my past and his. *(Pause.)* You are
        curious about what it was like. Like for us. Then.

PAUL: I am not listening.

MARK: Then leave.

PAUL: I -

MARK: You can't, can you?

(Silence. PAUL moves back into the centre of the room.)

PAUL: Alex will be back soon. Then we'll go.

MARK: And your case is ready. That's another thing.
        He'll be surprised you haven't taken some of the
        luxuries I have given you over the years.

PAUL: I want to go lightly.

MARK: Alex likes luxuries. He knows you had them
        from me. He won't be altogether happy with just
        you and not those little extras.

PAUL: Any moment he will be back.

MARK: And until he is I am here with you, and I want to
        tell you things. *(Pause. MARK looks intently at
        PAUL.)* Alex and I were happy. He was happy
        with me, for a while.

*(PAUL sits. He is completely motionless during MARK's
speech.)*

MARK: He was a good lover. But he wasn't perfect. He
        went off with other guys when he felt like it. I

suppose you do know that he is four years older than me? I know you may have noticed he looks younger, but then he wasn't fighting for his life, or fighting the fear that his life would be taken from him. *(MARK sits down and faces PAUL, who chooses not to look at him.)* The night sweats. The diarrhoea. The loss of weight. He pretended not to notice at first, then the tenderness went, and all of the gentleness. He'd shout at me for making the bed wet with sweat. He still had sex with me, but violently as if punishing me for something he was afraid of. That's the truth. Whatever else he told you is lies. *(Pause.)* Neither of us would admit that I could possibly be HIV positive. You see we were like a lot of people in the middle of the epidemic. We refused to believe it could happen to us, and in a way we refused to believe it was happening to anybody else. Alienation is quite, quite possible under those circumstances. We alienated ourselves almost totally from the outside world. *(Pause.)* When friends or acquaintances got sick, or died, we knew it was Aids, but we didn't know. When we went into the clubs and pubs we didn't look at the health education posters. Sometimes if there was a hunky man on it we would look at the picture. Aids was so unreal it was unreal. *(Long pause.)* Until I really fell ill. Until I went into the hospitals. *(PAUL puts his head in his hands. MARK pulls them away from his face, and looks at his face.)*

MARK: It was like going through a dark tunnel. A tunnel that we knew we were trapped in. *(Long pause.)* Or I was trapped in.

(PAUL gets up slowly. Goes towards the exit. Once more he cannot leave.)

PAUL: He'll be back soon.

MARK: Then you will be free.

PAUL: Yes.

MARK: I was so afraid, Paul. Very afraid. *(Pause.)* He tested, and he tested negative. He left me.

PAUL: *(Slowly.)* I must leave.

MARK: *(Asks the same question six times, each time his voice rising to an almost unbearable pitch.)* Why? Why? Why? Why? Why? WHY?

PAUL: *(Cries out.)* I don't want your horror.

(Loud hammering on the door. SIMON enters. PAUL steps back, disappointed.)

SIMON: He sent me.

PAUL: *(Panic in his voice.)* Who sent you?

SIMON: Alex.

MARK: Where is he?

PAUL: Yes, where is he?

SIMON: He's already gone.

PAUL: Am I to join him in Paris?

SIMON: No.

PAUL: Why?

MARK: *(Begins to laugh.)* Twenty years later and he is repeating himself. That man has learnt nothing.

PAUL: Shut up, Mark.

SIMON: He has not gone to Paris. *(Pause.)* I gave him the money to go further. He has gone to New York. *(Smiles at MARK.)* Seems that even after twenty years in gay Paris he still couldn't speak the language properly. *(Turns to PAUL.)* Didn't want to show himself up as a fraud to you, Paul.

PAUL: What am I going to do?

SIMON: Won't Paris do alone?

PAUL: No.

SIMON: Pity.

MARK: I won't say goodbye to him. I shouldn't, but I care about that.

PAUL: *(Shouts.)* I don't care about your goodbye, what about my own? You did this Mark. You paid him to leave me so that I would stay with you. *(Turns to SIMON.)* Isn't that true, Simon?

SIMON: Don't be ridiculous.

PAUL: He wouldn't have left me. There's something more I don't know about.

SIMON: Such as?

PAUL: He said he loved me.

SIMON: *(Laughs.)* You idiot.

PAUL: *(To MARK.)* Don't think you've got me. I won't stay.

SIMON: Personally, I don't want you to stay. I can't speak for Mark.

MARK: Paul, you will do what you want to do.

PAUL: *(To SIMON.)* Where will he be in New York?

SIMON: How should I know? Maybe he'll be sitting on top of the old Empire State Building waiting to become a millionaire.

PAUL: You must have some idea.

SIMON: I just gave him - *(Long pause.)* - the money.

PAUL: Well, I will follow him.

SIMON: I won't give you the money.

MARK: Stop it, both of you. *(Quietly.)* Don't either of you understand that I still love him? Yes, it's true. Still. *(Pause.)* Oh, he was changed. But he was the same, and there was enough of the same there to love.

PAUL: You hated him for what he did to you. And anyway, he hated you.

MARK: It doesn't matter. You don't hate in return because you are hated.

PAUL: I hate him.

SIMON: *(As if talking to a child.)* There, there. You'll recover. It's not a fatal disease, hating, Paul.

MARK: Will you both, please, leave me alone? *(Turns to PAUL.)* Use your freedom, make your choices. I am still here if you want my help.

PAUL: I don't want you.

MARK: We'll see.

(PAUL exits.)

SIMON: Maybe I did wrong, giving him that money. Alex didn't really want to return to Paris.

MARK: It's not important.

SIMON: I thought it best. I don't know why.

MARK: I understand.

(Stage lights soften. The change in lighting should denote a brief passing of time. MARK looks around him as if seeing the surroundings for the first time. He then looks at SIMON.)

MARK: He has gone, hasn't he?

SIMON: Paul?

MARK: *(Shakes his head.)* Alex. Somewhere in New
York. What do you think he's doing there? And
why did he come back after all these years?
(Looks again at SIMON who turns away.) So
many questions. Perhaps I didn't ask the right
questions. *(Long pause.)* I wonder too what he
did the day we celebrated the victory over the
virus. It's always intrigued me, what he did then.
(Pause.) Alex, who has always been elsewhere.

SIMON: I know where I was. I was in the hospital. *(Walks
slowly over to MARK.)* I saw what happened
there. Inside.

MARK: Sit down with me. Please. I feel cold.

SIMON: *(Sits next to MARK. Takes MARK's hand and
strokes it tenderly.)* You'll get warmer. It'll be
better now.

MARK: We've never talked about it much. That day. Me
outside. You inside. What it was like for us.
Maybe now it's time to remember.

SIMON: The struggle didn't end for us then, did it?
(Pause.) I feel it has now.

MARK: Peaceful. *(Long pause.)* Peace.

*(MARK and SIMON look at each other. Blue light begins
to slowly fill the stage.)*

MARK: The balloons went up first. It was a magnificent
sight. White and blue balloons rising up into the
sky.

SIMON: I didn't see it.

MARK: The crowds cheered as they went up. It was like
it would never end the number of people there on
the ground, men, women, children, releasing the

balloons into the air. *(Pause.)* I bought a balloon. I chose blue for you as I knew it was your favourite colour. You see, I didn't know then if you would survive. I had heard about the complications, and this gift for you was my prayer for you to live. *(Short pause.)* As I let it go, I said: 'I love you my friend'.

SIMON: I got well so quickly.

MARK: *(Gently.)* I know.

SIMON: *(Strokes MARK's hand, then takes his hand away. He clasps them tightly in front of him and his body stiffens a little. He doesn't look at MARK, but stares ahead.)* On the ward liberation hadn't the same meaning. (Pause.) A lot inside knew it was too late. Thousands and thousands were dying, gone past any point of cure. Some went mad with despair, knowing that comrades less ill than themselves would get well, be free, while they would have to die.

(Silence. MARK puts his head into his hands.)

SIMON: There was this boy on the ward. Sixteen years old. His face was covered with lesions. He never looked at his face in mirrors. *(Pause.)* That day of liberation he asked for a mirror. *(Slight pause.)* He smashed the mirror against the iron of the bed. And taking the broken glass, cut at the sores. He slashed and he slashed at his face. He was screaming: 'Let me die. I don't want them to try to make me well. I don't want any more torture. Let me die.' *(Long pause.)* They had to restrain him. It took three men to do it. He didn't stop screaming as they dragged him from the ward. Much later he was brought back on a stretcher. His face had been bandaged, and he was in a drugged sleep. *(Slight pause.)* He woke

up late that night to the sound of fireworks
outside. He yelled out once: 'I am not dead.'
(Pause.) For the remainder of the time I was on
the ward he was there, but he never cried out
again, and he never, never uttered another word.

MARK: *(Takes his hands away from his face. He has
been crying.)* I -

SIMON: Shhh. Be quiet. No more words.

MARK: I - I'm -

SIMON: Shhh.

*(MARK is silent. SIMON reaches for his hand and MARK
holds it tightly.)*

SIMON: *(As if finally.)* We must think of the future.

MARK: *(Quietly.)* I'm afraid.

BLACKOUT

END OF PLAY